MAKING HUMOR WORK

Take Your Job Seriously and Yourself Lightly

Terry L. Paulson, Ph.D.

CRISP PUBLICATIONS, INC.
Los Altos, California

MAKING HUMOR WORK
Take Your Job Seriously and Yourself Lightly

Terry Paulson, Ph.D.

CREDITS
Editor: **Michael G. Crisp**
Designer: **Carol Harris**
Typesetting: **Interface Studio**
Cover Design: **Carol Harris**
Artwork: **Ralph Mapson**

Copyright © 1989 by Crisp Publications, Inc.
Printed in the United States of America

Crisp books are distributed in Canada by Reid Publishing, Ltd., P.O. Box 7267, Oakville, Ontario, Canada L6J 6L6.

In Australia by Career Builders, P.O. Box 1051 Springwood, Brisbane, Queensland, Australia 4127.

And in New Zealand by Career Builders, P.O. Box 571, Manurewa, New Zealand.

Library of Congress Catalog Card Number 88-72262
Paulson, Terry L.
Making Humor Work
ISBN 0-931961-61-0

PREFACE

When a comedian uses humor, we're always asking 'Is it funny?' When you use humor in the business world, the question is different. You are asking—'Does it work?''' That comment, shared by Gabe Cohen, a former Second City comedian, accomplished actor, and co-presenter at a HUMORWORKS Seminar, helped define the unique purpose of this book.

This is not another book to make you laugh. You will laugh, but that's not the purpose. It is designed to introduce you to the value of humor and how you can learn to use it on the job to increase not only your personal and professional effectiveness, but also the effectiveness of others.

Making Humor Work is a friendly, practical guide. You will learn how humor unlocks the receptivity of others and helps to enhance communication.

You will be shown how humor can disarm anger and defuse resistance to change while still promoting problem solving.

Perhaps, most important, you will learn how humor can help you develop more self-confidence and manage stress in a changing world.

Humor can help your organization run smoother, cut medical costs, increase sales and production levels, and even polish the company's public image.

A benefit on any job is laughter. It should never be a crime to have fun on the job; it may very well be a crime not to. And best of all, it doesn't cost a penny.

Making Humor Work is not a book to be read once and deposited on a shelf. It is a book to return to for refueling about how to keep humor your ally on the job. Enjoy it and enjoy it again. And now, let there be laughter, and let it begin with you.

Terry L. Paulson, Ph.D.

i

ABOUT THIS BOOK

Making Humor Work is not like most books. It has a unique ''self-paced'' format that encourages you to become personally involved in a unique discovery of the value and effectiveness of humor. It was designed to be read with a pencil. There are exercises. There are quotes that invite being underlined. Mark it up and make it yours.

Making Humor Work (and the other self-improvement books listed in the back of this book) can be used effectively in a number of ways. Here are just some possibilities:

Individual Study. All you need is some time alone. You pick the location. Pull the covers over your head, turn on your flashlight, and be ready to learn and to laugh.

''The illiterate of the future are not those that can not read or write, but those that can not learn, unlearn and relearn.'' Alvin Toffler, author of Future Shock.

In today's changing world, self-improvement is a badge of adequacy not inadequacy. Your sense of humor is one thing worth improving.

Workshops and Seminars. This book is ideal for pre-assigned reading prior to a workshop or seminar. With the basics in hand, workshops can expand on concepts and give people time to practice in groups.

Remote Location Training. Copies can be sent to those not able to attend ''home office'' training sessons.

Informal Study Groups. Thanks to the format, brevity and low cost, this book is ideal for short ''brown-bag'' or other informal group sessions. Humor is a popular topic in every company; this book gives you a chance to capitalize on that.

These in no way exhaust the possibilities for the use of this book.

TO THE READER

Making Humor Work is a not just another funny book to be read—it 's a book to use. Each chapter provides insightful information, provocative quotes, useful strategies, and practical exercises for upgrading your humor skills. These are the why, what, and how of making humor work. They all combine to reinforce and illustrate the key principles of the book.

Strategies That Work—Each chapter provides actual examples of how real people use humor to get results on the job. Suggestions you will be able to use immediately to make humor work for you are provided.

Provocative Quotes—Each chapter has quotes that will both inspire and inform. You will come to appreciate the breadth of support for the appropriate use of humor.

Exercises—Every chapter contains pencil exercises that invite participation. All it takes is a quiet place, some time, and the motivation to take practicing humor seriously. Involve others; humor benefits are contagious!

Keepers—All chapters end with a list of key points worth keeping. Without review, what we retain from even the best book is minimal. This book was designed to be read more than once. To make review easy, you can quickly reread the chapter ''Keepers'' to cement key points into your memory. What is reviewed is retained. Only material that is retained can be used! Some readers make audiotapes of their humor keepers—the quotes, the strategies, the key ideas that they want to work on. They then listen to their ''Humor'' tape on the way to work or somewhere else at least once a week. What you remember, no one can take away from you.

This book doesn't end your humor education; it's simply a good place to start. There is much more to learn about your sense of humor and how it can work for you. The ''Reference'' section provides some direction on how to keep your humor skills growing.

Enough! Now pick up your pencil, focus your eyes, and turn to Section 1.

ABOUT THE AUTHOR

Terry Paulson is one of America's top-rated professional speakers—and one of the busiest. In addition to being a licensed psychologist and author of the best-selling book, THEY SHOOT MANAGERS DON'T THEY?, he is also editor of *Management Dialogue*.

Dr. Paulson is President of Paulson and Associates, Inc. in Agoura Hills, California. He designs and conducts practical and entertaining programs for major companies such as IBM, Arco, Johnson & Johnson, 3-M, Nissan and Rockwell on topics ranging from self-motivation and time management to managing conflict and managing change.

Dr. Paulson can be reached at (818) 991-5110

CONTENTS

Preface   i

To The Reader   iii

I   Taking Your Job Seriously and Yourself Lightly   1

II   Self-Confidence and the Ability to Laugh at Oneself   13

III The Communication Edge   19

IV   Disarming Anger With Humor   29

V   Making Humor Work During Change   34

VI   Bridge Building   39

VII Using the Funny Side to Improve Sales   47

VIII The Humor Factor and Creativity   57

IX   Laughter May Be The Best Medicine   65

X   Review of Humor Keepers   71

XI   Appendix: References   75

"There are three things that are real—God, human folly and laughter. The first two are beyond comprehension. So, we must do what we can with the third."

John F. Kennedy

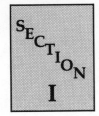

TAKING YOUR JOB SERIOUSLY AND YOURSELF LIGHTLY

HUMOR MAKES A DIFFERENCE

Most of us have become far too serious. We have people that are better trained than ever, but they don't seem to have nearly as much fun as they once did. U.S. workers, for example, consume over 15 tons of aspirin a day. As if our own personal and professional lives were not stressful enough, we are besieged with a steady diet of depressing local, national and world news.

The media guarantees to bring any world or national crisis to your doorstep the same day. If there are no catastrophes, do not despair. The networks have a ready supply of footage from old tragedies to celebrate anniversaries of pain. It's no better on the job; reorganizations, corporate buyouts, and world competition are causing workers to work harder, change, or fall behind. It is no wonder stress related illnesses are filling our doctor's offices.

As a result, many of us have lost touch with the importance of fun in the workplace. We move steadily through life with flat expressions on our faces. Take a minute and list the people on the job that look like they are in pain most of the day. Before you laugh too hard, think if others might put you on their list. It is dangerous to confuse professionalism with seriousness. You can take your job and your world seriously, and still take yourself lightly.

Human beings by nature are spontaneous and playful creatures. Yet the older we become, the less appropriate it seems for us to allow it to be expressed. We get "professionally" serious and then pay comedians to do a job we've forgotten how to do ourselves.

> "Laughter need not be cut out of anything, since it improves everything."
> *James Thurber*
>
> "Life is too serious to be taken seriously."
> *Oscar Wilde*
>
> "I deeply believe in humor; not in jokes. Humor is spectacular!"
> *Tom Peters*

THE HUMOR PARADOX

Consider the "Humor Paradox": Most of us were trained to put a lid on our humor, but we still tend to respect people who use it. We enjoy seeing charismatic people with a good sense of humor. Successful politicians make effective use of humor because it helps get them elected and helps keep them in office. People with a sense of humor are people you want to work with, listen to, and whose products you want to buy. Polls of company chief executives have found that they prefer to hire staff with a sense of humor. In our changing, challenging times, humor helps put the joy back in work. It helps keep a spring in your step.

SERIOUSNESS TRAINING

"Office congregating and merriment will not be tolerated in the future. . .Loud talking, laughing, loitering, and excessive walking are not mannerisms of true professionals."

Memo from a department manager of a large company

With statements like the above it is easy to understand why many have come to kill the playfulness that was so much a part of our childhood. Take a moment to look at your own "seriousness" training in the home and on the job. It is difficult to expand your humor potential unless you are aware of some of your internal self-blocks that have been programmed against its use.

EXERCISE: Identify Your Serious Training Messages.

"Wipe that smile off your face!"
"You think that's funny, don't you!"

What things were said in your home that may have suppressed your sense of humor?

1. _____

2. _____

3. _____

"Stop fooling around and get back to work!"
"We aren't paying you to socialize!"

What has been said on the job that has stifled humor and laughter on the job?

1. _____

2. _____

3. _____

You might ask if some 'serious' training isn't a good idea. The answer is emphatically, yes. There is more than a kernel of truth to the importance of taking some things seriously. Remember the theme of this chapter—Take your job seriously and yourself lightly. Making your work environment a "comedy store" is not making humor work; it is an abuse of an organization's time when important work is not being done. Work hard and laugh hard. Misplaced humor can be counterproductive and distracting. But life on the job or at home without laughter is also not the answer. When the time comes to get down to business, zip it up and get on with it.

YOU HAVE A JOB TO DO.
BUT YOU CAN HAVE FUN ALONG THE WAY

WHEN HUMOR DOESN'T WORK

> "Realize that a sense of humor is deeper than laughter, more satisfying than comedy and delivers more rewards than merely being entertaining. A sense of humor sees the fun in everyday experiences. It is more important to have fun than it is to be funny."
>
> *Lawrence J. Peter and Bill Dana*

Humor can be defined as that which makes us laugh, smile, or amuses us. Unfortunately, **not all humor works**. Humor can detract from a serious discussion. It can be used to deflect valid criticism. Some never-say-die comedians have been criticized for "never taking anything seriously". Balance again is the byword. Humor can be used to disarm anger, but it "works" for both parties only when it is used to go beyond the laughter and solve the problem that produced the anger.

SARCASTIC HUMOR

Some humor brings laughter at the expense of others. Instead of bringing people together, the use of sarcastic humor tends to keep people apart. Some people use sarcasm like a knife, inserting it quickly, turning it for effect, and then pulling it out before the victim realizes he or she has been stabbed. Sarcasm may work with close friends equally adept at its use, but it can also be dangerous. If you have participated in a poker group with six psychologists for ten years, it is probably O.K. to say a few sarcastic things, but this is based on years of friendship that gives a context of trust and caring to the "not so caring" messages. On the job, such comments are not appropriate. Even well-meaning sarcastic comments may be overheard by people who don't know their intentions.

ETHNIC HUMOR

Even more dangerous is the use of ethnic humor. Bias is too easy to ignite and too hard to kill. If you must use ethnic humor, make your own race or ethnic group the brunt of the jokes.

LAUGHING AT OTHERS

Laughing at others is rarely as appropriate as laughing at yourself or at a common experience. "We were having a great time laughing about our mistakes with the boss, but as soon as I joked about one of his, the fun went out of the conversation." If you must laugh at the situation of another, laugh instead at yourself through them by quickly sharing, "I'm sorry. I can't help laughing. It reminds me of the time I..." By becoming part of the situation, you can turn a potentially bruised ego into a warm smile. When humor is working, you laugh with people, not at them.

DRAWING THE LINE ON HUMOR

Take time to take a critical look at where you would draw the line on humor in the workplace. It is as important to explore your humor limits as it is for you to understand the potential for its use. Complete the exercise below.

EXERCISE: Where Is Humor Inappropriate On-the-Job?

List the situations you've seen humor used in a way that you thought was inappropriate:

1. _____

2. _____

3. _____

4. _____

5. _____

Don't Do This If Humor Is Inappropriate

DEVELOPING A STYLE OF HUMOR

"There are three rules for creating humor, but unfortunately no one knows what they are."

Laurence Peter

Humor has always been an expression of the freedom of the human spirit. It is an ability to stand outside of life's flow and view the whole scene—the incongruities, the tragedies outside our control, the unexpected. As an expression of individual freedom, each of us should work to develop our unique style of humor. Kill all clones. This book can help you find your personal unique humor style that will make you more effective and allow you to have more fun on the job.

What you get from this book will be different from other readers. Some things will be "old hat;" and some things won't fit. You wouldn't be caught dead doing some things this book suggests. You'll recognize those areas when you find yourself wiggling your eyebrows rapidly and humming the theme music from "The Twilight Zone." But some ideas should excite you and inspire you to the legitimate value of humor in the workplace. That's the challenge of this book—to find your personal message. It starts by understanding your "Humor Quotient" on the facing page.

It's hard to have a destination if you don't know your starting point.

EXERCISE: How Humor Works for You

It's too easy to take your sense of humor for granted. You may be humorous and not know it unless you take time to understand how humor helps you at work. List four ways humor works for you on the job:

1. _____

2. _____

3. _____

4. _____

DETERMINE YOUR HUMOR QUOTIENT

EXERCISE: Your Humor Quotient

Read the statements and circle the number where you feel you belong. If you circle a 7, you are saying the statement is "very characteristic of you" (True—Could not improve!); if you circle a 1, the statement is "very uncharacteristic of me" (Not me—I may need a "humor transplant!"). Be honest—No one is watching!

1. My boss would describe me as a "Humor Asset;" because my sense of humor benefits the company.   7 6 5 4 3 2 1

2. My co-workers and family would list my sense of humor as one of my best assets.   7 6 5 4 3 2 1

3. I avoid sarcasm, ethnic or negative humor except in private conversations with close friends.   7 6 5 4 3 2 1

4. I can laugh at my own mistakes and enjoy occasionally being poked fun at.   7 6 5 4 3 2 1

5. I laugh alone when I feel something is funny.   7 6 5 4 3 2 1

6. As a humor consumer, I easily laugh and enjoy laughing at jokes and stories others share.   7 6 5 4 3 2 1

7. I seek out cartoons, comedy shows, comedians and other humor stimulants.   7 6 5 4 3 2 1

8. I write down humorous stories and keep cartoons and articles that promote humor.   7 6 5 4 3 2 1

9. When stressed on the job, my sense of humor helps me keep my perspective.   7 6 5 4 3 2 1

10. I spontaneously look for the funny side of life and share it with others.   7 6 5 4 3 2 1

11. I send humorous notes and cartoons to friends, co-workers, and customers.   7 6 5 4 3 2 1

12. My sense of humor makes it hard for people to stay mad at me.   7 6 5 4 3 2 1

13. I love to tell humorous stories to make my point in on-the-job communication.   7 6 5 4 3 2 1

14. I sometimes act silly at unexpected times.   7 6 5 4 3 2 1

15. I am not uncomfortable laughing out loud with coworkers.   7 6 5 4 3 2 1

16. I use humor to help myself and others recall important things.   7 6 5 4 3 2 1

If you score 100-112, you are lying or can't add; a score between 90-99, indicates "Humor Pro"; a score of 70-90 means minor adjustments may be in order; a score of 45-70 suggests a major adjustment is needed (read this book at least twice!); a score below 45 may require a "humor transplant". If you did not laugh or smile at this scoring, give yourself a zero!

WHERE DOES YOUR HUMOR COME FROM?

EXERCISE: Exploring Your Humor History

You carry a reservoir of humor with you wherever you go. Unfortunately, few of us take time to enjoy the library of humorous memories stored neatly in a corner of our brain. Take a few moments to journey down the funny side of your past. List your funniest . . . :

Movies: _____

TV Shows: _____

Candid Camera or Blooper Show Scenes: _____

Jokes: _____

Relatives: _____

Friends: _____

Boss: _____

Co-workers: _____

Sales Experience: _____

If you couldn't think of any examples, you've lost touch with your humor history. Taking time to relive your humor history can be an energizer. You can't use it if you don't remember and review it frequently.

"Nothing is better than the unintended humor of reality."

Steve Allen

"Humor is what makes people laugh,"

P.G. Wodehouse, British humorist

"Humor is a way of looking at something that makes it funny."

Jack Smith, L.A. Times Columnist

"LIFTERS" AND "POPPERS"

Working the funny side of life is an adventure in creativity. You get what you look for in life. Are you looking for opportunities daily to say, "That's funny!"? You should be!

Invest time developing two sources of humor—"the lifters" and "the poppers." You won't develop them; you'll have to keep them. Start by buying yourself your own humor storehouse.

Your Humor Shopping List

If you're ready to get serious about making humor work, here's what you need to get started:

A Laughter Log (a humor notebook, otherwise known as a spiral notebook)

A Humor File (otherwise known as an index file or a manilla folder—colored for those who live dangerously)

A Humor Album (otherwise known as a picture album)

Now you have a place to keep what you find. You'll need to start first with collecting "lifters"—That is..."lift" any examples of humor you hear, see, or read. The first rule to developing your sense of humor is simple—"If you like it, save it." The palest pencil mark is better than the best memory. Write down anecdotes and stories you could see yourself using on the job. Collect cartoons, advertisements, pictures, and articles that make you laugh and that relate to your work, products or services. By looking for and collecting humor, you open your eyes to the humor all around you.

Once you've started collecting, leave space for the "poppers," because they are sure to follow. When you look for, read, and collect humor, you will find that humorous thoughts and spontaneous witty statements will "pop" into your mind at the most unusual times. That's how an emerging sense of humor grows.

Have paper available to write "poppers" down at your most creative moments. Cultivate humor with these mental openers—"What if..." or "Do you ever wonder..." By opening the mind to crazy humor options, you are feeding your mind humor fuel.

Given ample time to relax, your own humorous ideas will start to come. The thoughts will come, but don't let your early serious training stifle them. Don't consider such thinking "frivolous." You have a right to enjoy life, and such thinking will sharpen your mind. Don't stifle humor; fertilize it!

OLD DOGS AND NEW TRICKS

''You don't stop laughing because you grow old; you grow old because you stop laughing.''

Michael Pritchard

You've heard the saying ''You can't teach an old dog new tricks!'' That's not true; old dogs can learn new tricks. Try a more accurate adage that a small motel showed on a sign that said: ''You become an old dog when you stop doing new tricks.'' Age is not a limiter. People learn to drive at all ages. They learn to drive because it's a long way to walk. It is also a long walk through life without humor as a sidekick.

You can always be a humor consumer; finding people to laugh along with is as important as creating humor. As a result, there is no promise that you will become a comedian after reading this book; that's not the goal. You will however, build a better batting average at using humor on the job.

BE BOTH A HUMOR

CREATOR AND A

HUMOR CONSUMER

AVOID THE THREE P'S

PERFECTION, PROCRASTINATION, PARALYSIS

''Have Fun! Misery is Optional!''
Jean Westcott

''Humor is such a great gift—why leave it to chance?''
Joel Goodman

The only place that perfect people exist are in fictional books and movies. That's because errors can be edited out. In the real world, we muddle through without dress rehearsals or editors. As a result, if you use humor, you must learn how to handle an occasional ''bomb'' along the way. How many times have you struggled to decide whether a story was funny or stupid, only to discover that by the time you decided it was worth telling, the time for telling it had passed. Don't hold your sense of humor captive waiting for the perfect time or the perfect story.

PRACTICE, PRACTICE, PRACTICE

Trade the myth of perfection for the reality of the moment, and **practice, practice, practice**. Make it a point to tell one new story or joke a week to every person you talk to. This practice will help sharpen your delivery and imprint the story in your memory for future use. With practice you will never be perfect, but you will be better. Even if a story or joke doesn't work, you'll soon learn ''savers'' that will help you make a winner.

Humor puts people at ease. It's the great common denominator. Everyone likes to laugh. Everyone enjoys being with people who bring laughter with them. This book is humor all the way, but humor with a purpose. People laugh about things they care the most about. If you want to make people laugh, you have to hit them where they breathe and they live. Humor can be warm and tender. But the bottom line is—humor does work.

''Parsons, even in prosperity, always fretting; Potts, in the midst of poverty, ever laughing. It seems, then, that happiness in this life rather depends on internals than externals...''

Ben Franklin

''No one would have been invited to dinner as often as Jesus was unless he was interesting and had a sense of humor.''

Charles Schultz

REVIEW OF SECTION I

HUMOR KEEPERS WORTH KEEPING
(Check those with which you agree)

☐ When humor is working, you laugh with people, not at them.

☐ Don't hide in humor; use it.

☐ Take your job seriously and yourself lightly.

☐ Take time to relive your humor history.

☐ Work the funny side by using "the lifters" and "the poppers."

☐ Keep your humor history where you can find it—your laughter log, humor file, and humor album.

☐ Trade Perfection, Procrastination, Paralysis for Practice, Practice, Practice.

☐ Ask "Does it work?" not just "Is it funny?"

SELF-CONFIDENCE AND THE ABILITY TO LAUGH AT ONESELF

> "I couldn't be two-faced. If I had two faces, I wouldn't wear this one."
>
> *Abraham Lincoln*

A very successful speaker recently gave the following advice to other speakers. He said: "Don't be afraid to put some egg on your face early. By being able to laugh at yourself, you take yourself off the podium and put yourself onto the audience's level." Laughing at yourself need not be self-depreciation; it can be a very healthy acceptance of one's own humanness. ***Learn to laugh at what you do, without laughing at who you are.*** Remember, it's always easier to admit you made a mistake than to admit you are one.

> "What is a sense of humor? Surely not the ability to understand a joke. It comes rather from a residing feeling of one's own absurdity. It is the ability to understand a joke—and that the joke is oneself."
>
> *Clifton Fadiman*
>
> "Whatsoever you laugh at in others, laugh at in yourself."
>
> *Harry Emerson Fosdick*

Only the truly self-confident admit and learn from their mistakes. Research has indicated that up to 80% of professionals have "imposter feelings". They aren't imposters; most would be rated by their bosses as being effective at what they do. But inside, they say to themselves, "If anybody knew how much I don't know about what I'm doing, I'd be in deep trouble." So they dress for success and pretend. We all know people who live a lie. Even when caught in the middle of an error, they will deny it or blame others. They invest an immense amount of energy into making sure others do not find their faults. All too often, these are the same people that go secretly to a therapist, wear sunglasses and pay in cash.

THE ABILITY TO LAUGH AT ONESELF
(Continued)

LIVING THROUGH OUR DAILY QUOTA OF ERRORS

Let's face it. We all make our quota of errors. If you're like most people, you occasionally feel that the quota allowed for some days is hardly adequate. With the world challenging us to change at alarming rates, few of us have time to master a required skill before they change it again. No one can promise you will be immune from mistakes, but you can learn from the one's you do make. Being able to laugh at yourself helps let go of mistakes and bounce back to attack the problem anew.

Life is like a car with no brakes. If you spend too much time looking in the rearview mirror, you will probably hit a tree you could have seen out the front window. That's why the front window is bigger. Laughter helps you focus on your front window. It allows you to keep your perspective. The past is over and you can do nothing to change it. You can laugh or you can cry, but get on with life.

KILLING THE MYTH OF PERFECTION

> ''I am careful of the words I use from day to day to try to keep them sweet for I never know from day to day which ones I'll have to eat.''
>
> *Anonymous*

We attempted to kill the myth of perfection earlier. Now's your chance to shovel dirt on its grave. It would be nice if we had the ability to edit out life's errors, but we don't. Putting the myth of perfection to rest involves accepting our humanness and working to become better—not perfect. Take a minute to accept some of your basic faults. Some are annoying, but others are endearing. They are what make you unique. What are unique qualities or habits you have that help define you?

EXERCISE: Exaggeration

Identify two personal mannerisms (verbal or nonverbal) that you are known for. Take the time to act out and exaggerate those mannerisms with a friend or a colleague.

1. _____

2. _____

The Rich and Famous

''Columbus did not know where he was going. When he got back, he didn't know where he'd been. And he did it all on borrowed money. There's hope for all of us.''

Bumper Sticker

''I've written six books. Not bad for a guy who has only read two.''

George Burns

''I don't trust anyone who can't spell a word two ways.''

Mark Twain

LINES YOU CAN LIFT

The Plain and the Ordinary

''I hope I grow up to be the person my dog thinks I am.''

''I'm such a poor speller, my spell checker laughs at me.''

''The ability to be cool under fire is a great skill. I wish I had it.''

''Everything works well; it's just thicker than I want it to be.''

''Sure, I'm virtuous, but I'm not a fanatic about it!''

''I may not be able to sing, but I sure can't dance.''

''As I once told (name of famous person), I can't stand name dropping.''

''I'm so neat that when my wife gets up to go to the bathroom in the middle of the night, I make her side of the bed.''

''Please don't judge my ideas by my budget.''

EXERCISE: Filling in Your ''Blooper Log''

Develop your own ''Blooper Show''—It's your chance to make fun of yourself before others beat you to it. List two embarrassing incidents on the job for your ''blooper log.''

1. _____

2. _____

THE ABILITY TO LAUGH AT ONESELF
(Continued)

HOW SELF-DEPRECIATION WORKS

When you tell a story that pokes fun at yourself gently, it acts as a social lubricant that says, "Hey, this person is a human being. Someone is at ease with life, and we can feel the same way."

We are afraid of those without humor. The teller of a joke on oneself, is saying that "I realize there have been mistakes; they are real but not as important as some people would make them." It shows a basic understanding of limits. Self-depreciation in essence, is taking things seriously enough to joke about them. The laughter of others springs from the appreciation of that acknowledgement about any "critical" issue is often exaggerated.

The humanness of a joke on oneself is often contrasted with "puns". "Puns" are seldom effective in making listeners comfortable. They may get some laughs, but by their very construction, a speaker is saying, "Look how smart I am."

MAKING FUN OF YOURSELF HELPS OTHERS LEARN FROM THEIR ERRORS

Hidden problems become big problems. By being able to laugh at and share your errors, you invite others to admit and learn from theirs. It releases the damned up psychic power of secrecy. People respect managers who develop a "coping model" which allows them to bounce back from setbacks, over those who project a more distant, "masterful ideal."

Strategies That Work

Consider giving a standing ovation for heroic efforts in the face of a bad day. When you find out who is struggling, have that person stand and give him or her a standing ovation. Watch the smiles melt away the tension. Don't forget to ask for one yourself when needed.

One business owner put a large bill on the conference table and told his staff one of his recent errors and what he learned. He then gave his challenge, "Anyone who can top it gets the money." He had the trust of his staff. Each shared a recent error, that evoked laughter. The "winning error" earned the money and a lot of laughter. Beyond that, everyone present learned from each error discussed."

Cover-ups

Most "ad-libs" aren't really spontaneous. Professional comedians memorize good come-backs beforehand. These come-backs are known in the humor trade as "cover-ups" and "savers".

Cover-ups You Can Use

"Cover-ups" are used to soften common problems that all speakers and managers experience. Their comments seem spontaneous, but they are planned and practiced until they are automatic.

If the lights go out say: "Would someone tell the power company the check is in the mail."

After a mistake during a speech, pause and say: "Wouldn't it be great if speeches came with erasers (or a delete button)?"

When the lights blink consider saying: "Ok God, I'll change the subject."

If you hear applause from another room that is noticeable, remark: "Thank you. I appreciate your support."

When you hear a disruptive noise, say: "I didn't realize my mother-in-law was in town." or look upward, pause, and say, "If you don't like that topic, we'll change it."

Savers

"Savers" can help when your attempts at humor fail. Even if one of your best stories gets nothing but confused stares, don't get stuck with "flop sweat". Everybody will "lay an egg" now and then. Never just squirm and go on. It is better to acknowledge the fact that your story bombed. Perhaps the following "savers" can take the terror out of storytelling. Use those listed, but also prepare some of your own to use when needed.

Savers You Can Use

"I just threw that in. I should have thrown it out."

"I thought that would be a biggie." (Take out a file card and tear it up.)

"Too bad folks, that was the humor portion of the meeting."

"That's the last time I buy a joke from...(key member of staff who can take a joke)."

"Some of these I just do for me. Bear with me."

(Look at your notes), "It says here 'Pause for laughter.'"

After picking up a typing mistake on an overhead say, "We added that so you perfectionists would experience joy finding it."

EXERCISE: ''Cover-ups'' and ''Savers''

Make up three ''cover-ups'' or ''savers'' you could use on the job. What are your common distractions? What are your most common errors? Prepare relevant comebacks and try them out.

1. _____

2. _____

3. _____

To be successful ''rise early, work hard, strike oil.''

J. Paul Getty

''Laugh at yourself first, before anyone else can.''

Elsa Maxwell

REVIEW OF SECTION II

HUMOR KEEPERS WORTH KEEPING
(Check those that make sense for you:)

☐ Don't take yourself too seriously.

☐ Laughter provides perspective getting us quickly out of the rearview mirror and back into constructive action.

☐ Self-depreciating humor humanizes the speaker.

☐ Humor helps promote a management style that supports problem-solving.

☐ Don't worry about humor that ''bombs''. ''Savers'' will capitalize on your misfortune.

THE COMMUNICATION EDGE

SECTION III

"He deserves Paradise who makes his companions laugh."

Mohammed, The Koran

THE SIN OF BEING DULL

"People will pay more to be entertained than educated."

Johnny Carson

"When the teacher turns to the blackboard he yawns."

Japanese Haiku by Isan

"Education doesn't have to be fun, but it helps. When using humor to communicate information tell it serious, tell it funny, tell it serious."

Jean Westcott

People often ask if it is necessary to use humor as a speaker. A well-worked reply is most fitting—"Only if you want to get paid!" You may not be paid to speak, but all managers need people who will listen to what they have to say. Professional speakers use humor because it works. Like it or not, we live in the entertainment age.

If you can't find a way of keeping your message interesting, people will tune you out and go to another channel. Our growing information glut has been described as trying to sip water from a fire hydrant. Effective humor will unlock an audience's receptivity. Successful humor is a "grabber" that pulls people out of the noise to work at listening. A lot of excellent information is neither read, nor listened to. Like the proverbial tree that falls in the wilderness and makes no sound, many speeches are given but never heard.

Good communicators make communication fun. They touch each listener's heart, brain and funnybone. Reliance on only one avenue will diminish the effectiveness of the message. When you learn to touch all three in a rhythm that informs, inspires and entertains, your listener will never know what you will do next. Listeners are compelled to listen because, in the tradition of storytellers of old, if you learn to seduce the listener to stay on your channel by pacing and varying styles and content, you will never want for attention.

HUMOR AND THE ADRENALINE ADVANTAGE

> "Humor is an attention-getter and a safety valve."
>
> *Ron Zemke*
>
> "To get 'em listening, get 'em laughing."
>
> *Allen Klein*

Consider the following description of a physical reaction: "The neural circuits in your brain begin to reverberate. Chemical and electrical impulses start flowing rapidly through your body. The pituitary gland is stimulated; hormones and endorphins race through your blood. Your body temperature rises half a degree, your pulse rate and blood pressure increase, your arteries and thoracic muscles contract, your vocal chords quiver, and your face contorts. Pressure builds in your lungs. Your lower jaw suddenly becomes uncontrollable, and breath bursts from your mouth at nearly 70 miles an hour."

This is a clinical description of laughter. It sounds like a disease, but it describes a person who is sold on listening. By getting laughter from your listeners, you have activated them for influence.

You might plead, "But the topics I talk on are not humorous." High tech does not need to be dry tech! Be creative and you'll find a place for humor in any presentation.

Strategies That Work

Make your messages memorable. One company enlisted a ventriloquist to help get across the importance of security. As the ventriloquist walked around the company's offices, file cabinets and desks shouted, "Lock me!"

One of the most shocking openings to any speech may have been a sermon delivered to a conservative church by Henry Ward Beecher. He said "God damn Son-of-a-bitch!" followed by, "that is what I heard coming over to church this morning, so I am changing my sermon to speak on the evils of blasphemy."

One flight attendant got the attention of even the most seasoned flyers by starting with, "There are 50 ways to leave your lover, but only 8 ways to leave this aircraft. Find your exit before you find your lover." When she asked patrons to fill out evaluation forms on the flight she scored another ten. She said "If you liked your flight, this is Air New Zealand flight 437; if you didn't, it is Quantas Flight number 29."

> "All I'm trying to do is show where humor fits in. It's not a yuk a minute. It's not a bunch of jokes. It forces you to think about every point you're going to make during a speech. All (humor) does is reinforce traditional practices but in a more pleasant, fun kind of way...."
>
> *Malcolm L. Kushner*

How many times have you attended meetings where people were using so much jargon that no one had any idea what was being said? Often in this situation, people just nod their heads. True communication provides more than a stream of words; it evokes images that help people understand and retain information. Effective communicators are not humorists; they only use humor. Their humor supports and illustrates a central message. By mixing substance with humor it is possible to get your message across and have your listeners enjoy the process.

A good story not only illustrates a point, it also gives listeners a memory hook to recall information. Research indicates that 85% of what we retain is visual. A good story builds a visual image with words. It prompts the listener to say "I've been there!" or "It could happen to me!" When they remember your funny story, they retain your point along with it. Using humor makes your serious points memorable. Your listener may laugh for only five seconds, but they'll think for five minutes on the meat of your message each time they remember it. As one manager put it, "I can give 'AhHa's' through 'HaHa's'."

INTERNATIONAL HUMOR

Using humor outside of your own country is not always easy, but it can be an asset. A good humorous example that illustrates a point by capitalizing on a common human foible is usually safe. Cartoons can be especially effective because they are visual and their themes are often international. If cartoons reinforce your point, test them on individuals before using them in groups.

Whatever medium of humor you use, take the time to simplify your story and remove colloquial phrases that would be hard to translate. Try out your stories to see whether they still fit before you use it with important business contacts.

> Art Gliner warns some international listeners will take your jokes literally. "A midwestern executive sent a cable to one of his Peruvian managers: send me office and factory headcount broken down by sex. Reply: 249 in factory, 30 in office, three on sick leave, none broken by sex—our problem is alcohol."

Always ask colleagues in the country what not to joke about. Self-depreciating humor is usually safest but may not be appropriate in some cultures. Be cautious. Even when humor is accepted, some countries are not used to hearing anything funny from a speaker. Let your audiences know that it is ok to laugh. By setting the stage for fun, you save the embarrassment of laughing alone.

KEEP YOUR HUMOR "ON TARGET"

If a joke or story has no point, leave it to the comedians. Humor that works and is on target progresses the message of the communicator. Start asking yourself: Does my story provide meaningful commentary? Will it be a bonus that moves my message along? Does it tie into my main point? Is it pertinent? Remember, even a good story can't be substituted for a good central message. Make humor work in carrying your message or save the story for the lunch room later.

Strategies That Work

In business, low risk humor is on-target humor. Following are some anonymous, on-target humor statements from managers that make a point. Read them to see if you get the message. If you do, feel free to use them to make a point in your activities.

"Do you like to travel? Do you want to meet new friends? Do you want to free up your future? All this can be yours if you make just one more mistake."

"50% of being smart is knowing what you're dumb at."

"Society is composed of three kinds of people: a few who make things happen, many who watch things happen and the majority—who have no idea what happened."

"Any person who says it can not be done should not interrupt those who are doing it."

"If you want to win the race take the time to look at the map. Following others can never be the strategy for those who want to win."

EXERCISE: List Two "On-target" Ancedotes that Illustrate Important Points

Take another journey into your humor history to catch examples of how humor already works for you in communication.

1. _____

2. _____

The magical answer to making others laugh lies less in technique than in the three big P's—*Practice, Practice and Practice*. Practice won't make you perfect but it will make you better. Tell one joke a week to every person you have a few moments to talk to. If individuals laugh, so will those on the job. Learn from experience what lines and set-ups work. You will keep some and throw many away. Cement the good ones to memory and write them in your ''Humor Log''. When you practice telling your stories, following are some ''keepers'' worth remembering:

''If you can't hit oil in 20 seconds, stop boring.''
Larry Wilde

---

1. *Brevity is critical.* The average length of a story or joke is 15 seconds. Nothing kills a story like unnecessary length. It has been said that ''Brevity is the soul of wit.'' When it's short, even if people don't laugh, at least you haven't wasted too much of their time. Maintain tension by building your story quickly toward resolution. Never slow it down by giving unnecessary information or taking tangents. Twist your lines, juggle words around and chop until you have a tight, but funny story that works. Don't just keep it short; speak at a brisk pace and accelerate into the clear punch line.

2. *Work at both the set-up and the punchline.* Good storytellers develop their story by framing the humor with an effective but quick set-up. If the ''facts'' of the story set-up are not logical or realistic, the story won't work. Learn to personalize your stories by using names, locations and activities. It makes your stories warmer, more interesting and appealing. Lack of believability in your set-up will diminish the payoff for your punchline. A good set-up lets the humor sneak up on the listener, moving them from the predictable to the witty, often absurd, conclusion.

A really good story explodes into the punchline which is nothing more than the unexpected truth that twists reality slightly. A set-up is controlled, but you must **punch** the punch line. It's too easy for the novice storyteller to fade on the most important part—the punchline! If you emphasize anything, make it the close. In baseball terminology, a joke is a curve; it starts for the plate and then bends at the last minute fooling the batter. Good stories do the same thing by surprising the listener. A good set-up makes the surprise possible; a strong punchline makes listening to the set-up worthwhile.

3. *Master the pause.* Time your pauses. This will give your audience time to visualize the story and grasp the situation you are creating so that when you give the punch line or twist the story, the effect will be even more laughable. You may raise your eyebrows, look to the side and smile, or say, ''Well, then.'' As the pro's suggest, ''Don't step on your lines.'' When you finish a story, stop, smile and wait for a response. Too many novices don't pause long enough and move on before the audience has a chance to absorb, appreciate and laugh.

4. *Allow yourself to be silly.* Forget all that serious training you had as a child. Show that you enjoy spreading cheer. Stay focused on your listener's eyes to capture their attention and to build your confidence. If you are talking to more than one, look from face to face. You should strive to live out the word, ''neoteny,'' which means ''maturing but retaining childlike qualities.'' Good humorists let their ''child'' show for fun and profit. When you use humor, give yourself permission to be a ''ham'' and show your emotions. Exaggeration is a big part of humor. Let your face and gestures help paint the picture.

5. *Keep using your ''winners.''* Don't be afraid to use a story many times. You play hit tunes more than once. People like hearing a good story teller tell the same story again. Even those who have heard it will enjoy watching others experience the surprise. Never apologize for any story; you are giving a gift of laughter. You can even get the benefits of the laughter from an earlier story by repeating your punchline again at strategic points in the same talk. Such punchlines are called ''anchor statements''. They bring back a common humor history, reinforce the theme, and invite another dose of laughter.

Anchor statements stretch the impact of positive, on-target humor stories. Whenever you hear someone say, ''It's an inside joke,'' after laughing, you'll know an anchor statement has been used.

> ''When someone blushes with embarrassment..., when someone carries away an ache..., when something sacred is made to appear common..., when someone's weakness provides the laughter..., when profanity is required to make it funny..., when a child is brought to tears...or when everyone can't join in the laughter..., it's a poor joke!''
>
> *Cliff Thomas*

6. *Know the difference between public and private humor.* If you must use ethnic, sexual or regional humor, make it at the expense of **your** ethnic group, **your** sex, or **your** region. If you are from Southern California, you can say, ''others believe the U.S. is tilted and all the nuts roll down to our end of the country. I don't think so; it's just that our weather is so good, all our nuts are outside.'' Make fun of your city but getting a laugh is never worth putting down any group. Offended listeners seldom appreciate even good ideas.

7. *Use a humor sandwich.* Learn to use the sandwich technique to keep your unforgettable stories on target. Tell the point you want to make, then give it back in the form of a humorous story illustrating that point. Finally, button it up by restating it again in a memorable way. Redundancy helps hammer home your message on all the channels available.

FINDING ON-TARGET HUMOR

Remember, in the business world it is essential to keep your humor on target. Develop a list of frequently used topics and key words that will help you search for and remember jokes and stories for the appropriate time. Such pre-planning helps you find relevant humor and allows the commonly heard transition statements, ''Speaking of...'' or ''How many of you have heard...''

How do you get material for stories? You can find it everywhere when you're looking for the ''funny side''.

Go to your local library and look through the humor books that are available. Skip those that aren't funny, aren't you, or aren't appropriate.

Write out those you can adapt. When you find a story you like, don't simply take it. Update it, personalize it, and shape it for your use. It is more important for anecdotes to be believable than to be true. If it enhances your message, you are serving your listener by using it. They don't have to be knee-slappers to use; they must, however, ring true to you. Take heart in the words of Jerry Clower who said: ''I don't tell funny stories; I tell stories funny.''

Purists need not limit their search to books. Collect funny experiences from your life. Write the punch line down and then weave back through the story, writing set-up material that is relevant. The next time you are waiting in line with nothing to do, take a playful trip back through your humor history. Use the misadventures of your childhood, your first love, your pets, your first job, oddball friends and relatives. Your reservoir of stories should be endless. Always work your own humor history first. The best humor is genuine humor and it is easiest to find genuine humor in your own experience.

Read the newspapers carefully. Life is funny and papers tend to catch it. Look for the funny side, cut out articles that amuse you and put them in your humor album.

EXERCISE: Learning from Your Humor Heroes

Never stand in awe of any comedian; learn from all of them you enjoy. Think of your favorite comedians and identify one of their characteristic voice qualities or mannerisms that you would like to make yours. What would you beg, steal or borrow from your comedians' story telling styles?

1. _____

2. _____

HOW HUMOR CAN GET YOUR MEMOS READ

Memos are a great place to practice the effectiveness of well-placed humor. Interspersing and ending memos with on-target, but humorous statements or anecdotes is wonderful. There is no timing necessary here. Humorous memos are read; kept and shared. In the paper glut we are all part of, well-placed humor will surprise and entice people to read the whole thing. The memo dispenses information as the reader searches for your next humorous gem.

CLASSIC HUMOROUS MEMOS

How to Understand Engineering Vocabulary:

It is in process—It means things are so wrapped up in red tape that the situation is hopeless.

Consultant (or Expert)—It is an ordinary person who is more than 50 miles from home.

Under consideration—Means...they have never heard of it.

Under active consideration—Means...we're looking for it in the files.

Reliable source—Is...the guy you just met.

Informed source—Is...the guy who told the guy you just met.

Will advise you in due course—Means...if we figure it out, we'll let you know.

Submitted by David Harrington, Director of Medical Engineering at the New England Medical Center.

Use Humor to Get Your Memos Read

CLASSIC HUMOROUS MEMOS (Continued)

Halley's Comet Has a Special Visit

An insurance carrier shared this series of memos on ''Halley's Comet and the Communication Gap.''

President to Vice President: ''Tomorrow, at approximately 9:00 p.m., Halley's Comet will be visible in this area, an event which occurs only once every 75 years. Have all employees assemble in the parking lot and I will explain this rare phenomenon to them. In case of rain we will not be able to see anything, so assemble in the cafeteria and I will show them films on it.

Regional Directors to Office Managers (two memos later): ''By executive order of the president, tomorrow at 9:00 a.m. the phenomenal Halley's Comet will appear in the cafeteria. In case of rain in the parking lot, the president will give an order, something that takes place only once every 75 years.''

EXERCISE: Create Your Own Humorous Memo

Pick a company policy or procedure that's worth poking fun at. Let your humor have a free reign in creating a brief new memo worth reading in the space provided below.

REVIEW OF SECTION III

HUMOR KEEPERS WORTH KEEPING
(Check those you intend to use)

☐ Communicate with substance and style.

☐ Good communicators touch their listeners in three ways—their heart, their brain, and their funnybone.

☐ Give 'AhHa's' through 'HaHa's.'

☐ Humorous illustrations provide ''attention grabbers'' and ''memory hooks'' for retention.

☐ Practice won't make you perfect, just better.

☐ Tell one joke or story a week to every person you have time to talk to.

☐ Keep your humor brief and fast-paced.

☐ Work at both the set-up and the punchline.

☐ Master the pause.

☐ Allow yourself to be silly.

☐ Keep using your ''winners.''

☐ If you must use sexual, ethnic, or questionable humor, keep it off the job.

☐ Use a ''humor sandwich''—Tell it serious; tell it funny; tell it serious.

☐ Keep your humor on target—Use the common transition statements, ''Speaking of...'' or ''That reminds me of...''

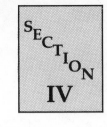

DISARMING ANGER WITH HUMOR

''If you want to rule the world, you must keep it amused.'

Ralph Waldo Emerson

''Why humor? Why not humor? I'd rather it be my ally than my enemy.'

Robert Orben

''Before you embark on a journey of revenge dig two graves.''

Booker T. Washington

''Gaiety is the most outstanding feature of the Soviet Union.''

Joseph Stalin

''Though a humorist may bomb occasionally, it is still better to exchange humorists than bombs. And...you can't fight when your laughing.''

Jim Boren

Few consultants these days talk about conflict resolution. It is now called conflict management. The message is that you don't get rid of conflict in a dynamic, changing world; you use it. Humor can help you manage conflict. Laughter is contagious; but so is negativity. Which would you like to spread?

HUMOR AND YOUR INNER ATTITUDE

Your use of humor in conflict management starts as an inner attitude. Behind every angry person is usually a problem that needs addressing. Confident people are not intimidated. Instead they want to move quickly beyond the anger to initiate productive problem-solving.

One successful manager keeps her perspective when handling angry customers by imagining a panel of judges awarding her points for her ability to handle a problem and the difficult customer. There are two scores for each judge: A form score and a degree of difficulty score. Mentally imaging that comical scene helps her avoid emotional reactions herself.

Others have been successful visualizing different, yet equally gratifying, scenes. A mild-mannered sales clerk imagines himself in a clown outfit suddenly choking an angry customer. A teenager thinks about telling a parent how much she appreciated being disciplined. An irritated employee imagines the boss lecturing him in his underwear. The effect was always the same. Instead of a snarl, a smile is possible even in difficult situations.

> "Go for the jocular vein, not the jugular vein."
>
> *Joel Goodman*

Verbal Aikido can be funny and effective. Instead of overpowering others with anger or arguments, take advantage of the jocular vein! Using positive empathetic humor instead of counterattacks, is one of a humorous application of the martial arts form of aikido. One of aikido's principal tenets can be summed up in two sentences—"When pushed, pull. When pulled, push." In verbal aikido the message is similar—"When attacked, accept, redirect, and affirm." Instead of giving an expected response of defensiveness ("Who me?") or the counterattack ("You're not so hot either!"), the attacker is turned aside by absorbing and using his attack—"You're right! It's not like me, but sometimes I act that way." One can honor the other person's right to a critical point of view while still maintaining one's own integrity and value.

Robert Kennedy was able to use his humor to soften the reaction to being appointed Attorney General of the U.S. by his brother. When asked his qualifications for the position, he replied, "If a person wants to become Attorney General, that person should first go to a good law school, study hard, get good marks, establish a reputation, and most important of all—have a brother who is President of the United States." You too can try your version of aikido. Could you use any of the following?

Aikido Strategies That Work

The Attack	*Aikido Response*
"It won't work!"	"You're probably right. There's no warranty on any idea. What problems do you see?"
"You're just like the rest of the managers around here!"	"I am a manager. It's reassuring that it shows. Now, what's the problem?"
"You women are all the same!"	"I'm glad you noticed. Now that we've settled that, what's the problem?"
"You aren't fair!"	"I'm sure sometimes I'm not. Help me understand how you see it."
"You're too young to understand."	"I'm as old as I can be for my age. What's the problem?"

An unexpected response absorbs and redirects anger in a harmless way without putting the other person down. Disarming anger should not be used to avoid problem solving. It should help us get through the emotional obstacles quickly. It's a blending with the aggressor instead of choosing to be aggressive or defensive.

Just as "savers" and "cover-ups" can be prepared for and practiced for the right time, you can develop comebacks that will turn snarls to smiles in even the toughest customers. Try some of the following with those tough situations.

Strategies That Work

"Yes, I'm the dummy you're yelling at!"

"Would you like to nail me to the wall now or later?"

"If I died, would that make you happy?"

"My name is. . .I never said it was God."

"I will never relinquish my right to screw up."

"I didn't do it, and I'll never do it again."

"Thanks, I needed that!"

"Is there anything else you don't like? I'm on a roll here."

"You don't like what I've done so far, and you're hoping the rest of my day will be at least as good."

"Hi! How did I destroy your morning?"

If someone is blatantly negative and you can't think of anything witty to say, try just saying "Thank you" and smile. This totally unexpected response is so outrageous and seemingly out of context that it is disarming. Some planning on your part will allow you to personalize some comebacks that are right for your job.

EXERCISE: Attacks and Comebacks

List three common attacks you hear on the job. Write a humorous punchline that you could use to deflect its sting.

Putdown	Comeback
1. _____	_____
2. _____	_____
3. _____	_____

CULTIVATING THE USE OF UNEXPECTED HUMOR

As previously mentioned, humor breaks the anger cycle. Properly done, it helps both parties move from confrontation to problem-solving. It should not be used to avoid a problem, but to help solve it. The complaint ''He won't take anything seriously!'' is not a compliment. Humor can be used to avoid dialogue. Problems will not go away with humor alone. Work as much at discussing viable solutions to the problem as you do at using your sense of humor to deflect the attack.

Strategies That Work

A CEO was chided by an irate stockholder for donating extensively to charities in a down year. When asked how much was donated, the CEO replied, ''Ten million dollars last year.'' The questioner mockingly said ''I think I'll faint.'' ''That might be helpful,'' the chairman replied, bringing down the house and regaining control of the proceedings.

Whenever the head of the personnel department had to face an irate administrator, she would greet them at the door with a fire hat perched on her head. They would look startled, smile, and ask, ''What is that for?'' She would say, ''Well, you told me it was an emergency!'' The tension was dissipated, and both could more easily address the problem.

One manager had a crisis meter on the door. The chart had a movable arrow with such readings as ''All is clear,'' ''Batten down the Hatches,'' and ''Meltdown.'' Once, as two managers intensified their argument, the manager went to the chart to change the meter reading. The resulting laughter helped refocus the conversation into constructive problem solving.

One manager found an interesting way to break the tension at a confrontational meeting. Just prior to starting the meeting agenda, he took out a target and pinned it to his chest to a chorus of laughter from the others in the room. The humor broke the tension and contributed to early problem solving.

Abraham Lincoln was a master in the use of humor. When challenged to a duel by a southern gentleman, he accepted under the condition he could pick the weapon and the location. After the gentleman accepted those conditions, Lincoln responded, ''Cow dung at five feet.'' You can guess the result.

BUILDING HUMOR BRIDGES NIPS ANGER IN THE BUD

You don't have to wait for an unplanned event to build humor into ''enemy'' relationships. It's often wise to plan ways to bridge the distance with humorous activities.

REVIEW OF SECTION IV

HUMOR KEEPERS WORTH KEEPING
(Check those with which you agree)

☐ You don't get rid of conflict in a dynamic, changing world—you use it.

☐ Behind every angry person's attack is a problem that needs to be dealt with.

☐ Instead of using counterattacks or defensiveness, ''verbal aikido'' uses positive empathetic humor to defuse verbal attacks.

☐ When attacked, accept, redirect, and affirm.

☐ Disarming anger should not be used to avoid problem solving.

☐ Develop and use comebacks that turn snarls to smiles in even the toughest customers.

☐ Don't hide in humor—Use it to promote problem solving.

34

MAKING HUMOR WORK DURING CHANGE

> "Everything is funny as long as it is happening to somebody else."
> *Will Rogers*

For most of us, change (especially if it is dramatic or unexpected) is like a shot a doctor forces us to have "for our own good." Like it or not, change is here to stay. We're in a fast moving vehicle with no brakes, and we're not even sure which map to use. If you agree that change is here to stay, you had better find a way to thrive within it. Humor can help us do just that.

THE ROLE OF HUMOR IN DEFUSING RESISTANCE TO CHANGE*

There will always be somebody who sees the negative side of change, such as the old farmer getting a look at his first car. He watched as the proud new owner cranked and toiled to no avail. The old farmer kept repeating to all that would listen, "It ain't gonna start." Once it started and the driver jumped behind the wheel, his message changed—"You ain't gonna be able to stop that thing!"

Resistance goes with the territory whenever change occurs. Not all resistance is bad: Some changes may be wrong. Resistance needs to be honored, listened to, and dealt with when this is the case. Effective leadership will admit when mistakes have been made and often poor changes can be reversed. But the normal early discomfort that accompanies change can often be handled by interjecting humor. This will keep people laughing at their new feelings of being uncomfortable. Instead of creating a defensive environment humor defuses the situation. It allows the acknowledgement that, "We're all in this together, and we're all uncomfortable."

Computer phobia provides a classic example of how change can be disabling for some. You probably know someone with "computer phobia." They are the ones who are afraid if they hit the wrong key the lights will go out. As they get training and develop mastery they move from tapping keys slowly to beating the sap out of the keyboard. But don't get cocky! Technology has a way of never letting you get comfortable. Just when you've mastered one system, there will be a new one to learn. Even those in the field have trouble keeping up. You've heard the difference between a used car salesman and a computer salesman; a used car salesman knows when he is lying.

In our changing world, when you rest, you rust. It requires living with a certain amount of uncertainty. When John Glenn, the first U.S. astronaut in space was asked what he thought about just before taking off into space, he said: "I looked around me and suddenly realized that everything had been built by the lowest bidder." You can laugh, or you can cry.

---

*For an excellent book read *Managing Personal Change* by Scott & Jaffe. See the order form at the back of this book for more information.

Change always brings uncertainty. Some companies have found ways to use humor to attack that uncertainty head on. In the ''Laugh Spot'' of an engineering department bulletin board, a company comedian posted this sign:

The Six Phases of a Project:

1. Enthusiasm
2. Disillusionment
3. Panic
4. Search for the Guilty
5. Punishment of the innocent
6. Reward and honor for the non-participants

Another company decided to use humor to deal with employee resistance to computers. They had each employee give names to their computers to personalize the machines. When you're frustrated with ''George'', not your computer, it was somehow easier to take it lightly. Workers would joke about problems with their ''George'' just as they would banter about another day with a frustrating spouse or boss.

At one large metropolitan hospital, the administration listened to their employees concern over lack of parking. After months of planning they announced construction of a new parking structure. But to build it, they had to temporarily take away valuable parking spaces. After initiating van pools and staggered schedules, there was still mayhem in the parking lots every morning. The personnel manager helped defuse the frustration of employees by publishing a list of parking rules in the following memo.

To: Employees
From: Management

Re: **Employee Parking Rules**

"Employees may participate in a demolition derby that starts in employee lots each morning promptly at 9:00 a.m. after all the spaces are filled. Employees who do not participate will automatically be declared losers."

"Employees who park illegally one time will be warned, after two times, will be stripped and flogged in front of other violators, and after three times, will be forced to eat all their meals in the employee cafeteria."

"Employees whose cars stick out in traffic lanes will have their rear ends painted red. If they continue to park this way, we will do the same thing to their cars."

Submitted anonymously from an employee at Huntington Memorial Hospital in Pasadena, CA.

"MURPHY'S LAW"

The list of Murphy's Laws that abound in every company are a testimonial to the importance at laughing at the real world of change. As Rosebeth Moss Kanter has said, "Every change looks like a failure in the middle." Here's a collection of laws that take advantage of humor in the midst of changing companies.

Laws, Rules and Other Truths

Finagle's Rules: Don't believe in miracles—rely on them.

Franklin's Law: Blessed is he who expects nothing, for he shall not be disappointed.

Navy Law: If you can keep your head when all about you are losing theirs, you don't understand the situation.

Probable Dispersal Law: Whatever hits the fan will not be equally distributed.

Runyan's Law: The race isn't always to the swift, or the battle to the strong, but that's the way to bet.

Truman's Law: If you can't convince them, confuse them.

Jones' Law: The man who can smile when all things go wrong has thought of someone he can blame it on.

Submitted by Joseph E. Drew, Jr., the jocular Director of Personnel with the Kern County Personnel Department, in Bakersfield, CA.

EXERCISE: Make Your Own "Murphy's Laws"

Using your name or the names of key staff, list three humorous laws that relate to your particular organizaton:

1. _____

    _____

2. _____

    _____

3. _____

    _____

One futurist confided that one of the six sources of future trend analysis he used was cartoons. He described cartoons as the quickest vehicle for getting into print what the populace is thinking about. What this person said makes sense. Humor can also help us make room for future-focused projectives. Take some time to develop some thoughts that communicate your vision of the future and how it will effect you, your company, and the economy.

EXERCISE: Your Nightly News Show for the Year 2010

Develop a news item for the year 2010 that relates to your work or issues that will effect it.

_____

_____

_____

Develop a commercial for the year 2010 promoting a product or service that projects your view of the future of our society. Come out with a slogan, a jingle, and a product or service name.

Name: _____

Slogan: _____

Jingle: _____

TAKING ADVANTAGE OF HUMOR WHERE YOU FIND IT

Sometimes, chance alone will provide an opportunity for humor to save the day in the midst of dramatic change. While discussing the loss of a major division in reorganization, the gloomy faces had spread across the entire conference room. When Jim went to pour coffee from the urn, he failed to watch the cup and continued to pour the coffee onto the table. Before he noticed, the President said with alarm, ''What do you think you're doing?'' Unable to stop in time, the coffee streamed off the table into his lap. He replied, ''What do you think I'm doing? I'm wetting my pants like everyone else.'' Everyone roared. It didn't soften the news, but it helped them get back to dealing with the changes while keeping their perspective. Don't leave humor to chance during these changing times; plan for it.

Paulson's Law: The people you most want to spend time with, you have to schedule to even see. The people you least want to spend time with will find you wherever you are.

REVIEW OF SECTION V

HUMOR KEEPERS WORTH KEEPING
(Check those which you support)

☐ Resistance goes along with the territory whenever change occurs.

☐ Not all resistance is bad; some changes should never even occur.

☐ Resistance needs to be honored, listened to, and dealt with.

☐ Use humor to handle the early discomfort of change—Laughing together allows all to say, ''We're all in this together, and we're all uncomfortable.''

☐ When you rest, you rust.

☐ Don't leave humor to chance in changing times—Plan for it!

SECTION VI

BRIDGE BUILDING

"Laughter is the shortest distance between two people."

Victor Borge

"You don't have to teach people to be funny. You only have to give them permission."

Dr. Harvey Mindess

Humor has always been an expression of the freedom of the human spirit, evidence of our capacity to stand outside of life and view the human condition. But as much as humor requires a free spirit, it also flourishes in a social setting. Laughter increases as social density increases.

William Hodge, a management consultant, surveyed 329 company executives and found 97% agreed humor is valuable in business, 60% felt a sense of humor helps determine the extent of an individual's business success. In an updated study, Hodge found 85% of chief executives (up from 45%) said that, "all things being equal, they would rather hire somebody with a sense of humor." In a similar study, a Burke Marketing Research survey found that 84% of personnel directors felt employees with a sense of humor do a better job than those lacking that quality. People not only value humor in employees, they also believe it works well enough to hire people that have used it.

Humor is one of the most frequently used social lubricants; it helps build quality relationships. Learning to foster the funny side of business can improve morale and increase team cooperation. People like to work with people that are fun. Laughter is contagious and so is negativism. Team-building managers have no doubt which mood they would like to spread.

Obviously, laughter is not the only way to boost morale. The number one motivator according to surveys remains the "work itself." One can't leave out the importance of effective challenges and recognition, but humor has its place. No one ever enjoys all aspects of a job, but looking at the funny side will help keep the tough parts palatable. The cheapest benefit on any job is laughter. It should never be a crime to have fun at work. People who work in an environment where fun is allowed want to come to work.

"If humor is accepted, you are probably in an environment where people are rewarded for the things they do, they are picked up after failures, and disagreements are settled more easily. If the humor level is down, that is probably also an indicator of how other things are settled."

Richard Davidson, Management Consultant

Making Humor Work

GIVE COMPLIMENTS THE HUMOR EDGE

With team members that deserve it, give compliments and add the gift of humor. We are not talking about sarcasm; we are talking about a sense of endearment.

''Joan is talented, intelligent, funny, warm and consistently cooperative. Outside of that, she doesn't impress me much.''

''As I look over this assembly of the finest thinking in our department, before we begin, I suggest we have Stewart say a short prayer.''

''Jim is a real misfit here; he gets along with everyone.''

One manager went beyond words. He had printed up coupon books that he gave employees for good performance. Examples included, ''Good for 10 minutes of silence—no matter how much your boss wants to keep arguing.'' ''Hand me this and I won't say, 'I told you so.''' The coupons helped keep the humor quotient high.

LAUGHING WITH INSTEAD OF AT OTHERS

You will occasionally run into situations where there is a serious problem for a co-worker, but the reality of the event is ''so funny,'' you can't hold back the laughter. You will quake in your shoes trying to show empathy to their plight, while you force back the smile uncontrollably forming on your lips. You will lose the battle more times than you would like to admit, but all is not lost. You can make laughing ''at someone'' laughing ''with them'' by immediately sharing a similar experience you have had. ''I'm sorry, That's funny! It reminds me of the time I...''

Successful people like me have
learned to laugh with others,
not at them

HUMOR GRAMS AND HOW TO KEEP THEM WORKING

Sometimes it seems like you can count on one hand the number of people that take time to express their appreciation directly. Most compliments seem to be given at going-away parties or at testimonials when employees die. Neither has a noticeable effect on the productivity of the employee being praised. Don't let this happen to you. Writing or sending a humorous note or card will show your appreciation and give the gift of laughter. Following is an example of a "Humor Gram" designed by the author. There is ample room to write a personalized note and a place to attach a handpicked, relevant cartoon.

We are
Please have a
humor break
□ **Happy**
on us!
□ **Sorry that...**

□ *You shared your suggestion with us.*
□ *You spread positive gossip about us.*
(We are even happier they listened.)
□ *We have to remind you.*
□ *You gave me such a warm reception.*
□ *You keep throwing business our way.*
□ *There was an ? to you.*
□ *You're in the "Good" News–*
Congratulations!
□ _____

So...

You need not be as elaborate. Your local stationary story will have plenty of "off the shelf" cards that reflect your humorous sentiments. Keep a number of them on hand to let people know you appreciate them.

Other possibilities include copying a favorite cartoon and using the copy as a letterhead for your note.

A leader's ability to use humor to persuade, encourage, and correct tends to breed an equality of status. When he or she allows mistakes to become a focus of fun-making instead of ridicule, that leader tends to bridge the gap between superior and subordinate. Humor is democratic rather than totalitarian.

EXERCISE: Design Your Own Humor Gram.

Write what you want included.

_____

_____

_____

_____

_____

_____

_____

TEAM BUILDING STRATEGIES CAN BE FUN

Think funny and adopt an attitude of playfulness whenever you are involved in team building. Remember to balance humor with appropriate seriousness. Humor is always an effective counterbalance to the hectic demands of achieving excellence. Take time to promote laughter. Smiling daily is a great start. Serious people are seen as distant, negative, arrogant, or intimidating. Do you want others to read that from your face as you walk the hallways? Try being creative in attempting some of the humorous teambuilding experiences shown on the next page.

Strategies That Work
(Check those you would consider adapting to your "team")

☐ On a regular basis, one hospital had a "silly hat day". Each worker, from top to bottom in the organization, was asked to wear a hat indicative of their job or their personality. They had a supply to assign for any who forgot. People learned it was better to bring their own rather than to risk having peers pick one for them.

☐ In a computer processing department, a "backrub break" was a daily lifesaver bringing relief and laughter. On a regular basis the supervisor would blow a whistle and a "backrub" tradeoff would begin.

☐ One manager loved to surprise people with catch phrases when projects were delegated. He loved to say, "Take this job and love it!"

☐ Preferring laughter to groans, one manager started delegating unpopular jobs by giving choices to his workers. She would delegate a usually unpopular project by giving her employees a choice between doing the project or an absurd job that was creative, hated, and funny. Her staff would always laugh but choose the project.

☐ One pharmaceutical company ended each Friday afternoon in the company cafeteria for weekly "Ho Ho's". It was off with neckties and on with fun at the regular social attended by as many as half of the employees. TGIF was truly a living reality in that company.

☐ One company started a TGIF-joke-network to end the week on a funny footing. On every Friday at 4:45 a person would start the chain with a joke and the others would call their chain partner with that week's joke.

☐ One manager locates photographs of famous people and puts them on the lounge board with a make-believe greeting from the celebrity to the staff for their fine work. It was always funny and timely.

☐ One manager made it possible for staff to "call in well" once a year. It meant you felt too good to come into work that day and needed a day to have fun.

☐ In Japan some CEO's have joined the national craze of singing along to a musical score of popular songs at company gatherings. When the CEO's tape their efforts, everybody joins in. There is team building laughter for all involved.

In a world with too many negatives, you can't leave the positives to chance. Build them into your department's daily routine.

EXERCISE: List Two Team-building Strategies for Your Company

1. _____

2. _____

BUILD A HUMOR HISTORY FOR YOUR ORGANIZATION

Look for humorous examples in memos, letters, meetings, and lunchroom gossip. Keep an album for your unit's humor history. Make a humor bulletin board, or "laughter spot," for workers to share cartoons, funny signs, anecdotes, and sayings. Save and share the best in your unit's humor album.

EXAMPLES WORTH POSTING

Taken from actual advertisements and signs:

"Caution: Blade Extremely Sharp! Keep Out of Children!"

"Dog for sale, eats anything, especially fond of children."

"Semi-Live Entertainment"

Taken from actual insurance accident forms:

"The guy was all over the road; I had to swerve a number of times before I hit him."

"I pulled away from the side of the road, glanced at my mother-in-law, and headed over the embankment"

"The pedestrian had no idea which way to go, so I ran over him.

Taken from actual welfare applications:

"Mrs. Jones hasn't had any clothes for a year and has been visited regularly by the clergy."

" I am glad to report that my husband who is missing is dead.

Taken from actual physician dictations:

"Patient died in his 90's of female trouble in prostate and kidneys."

"Discharge status: Alive but without permission."

"Both the patient and the nurse herself reported passing flatus."

MAKE YOUR OWN COMPANY FLOW CHART FOR A HUMOR BREAK

PROBLEM SOLVING TECHNIQUE

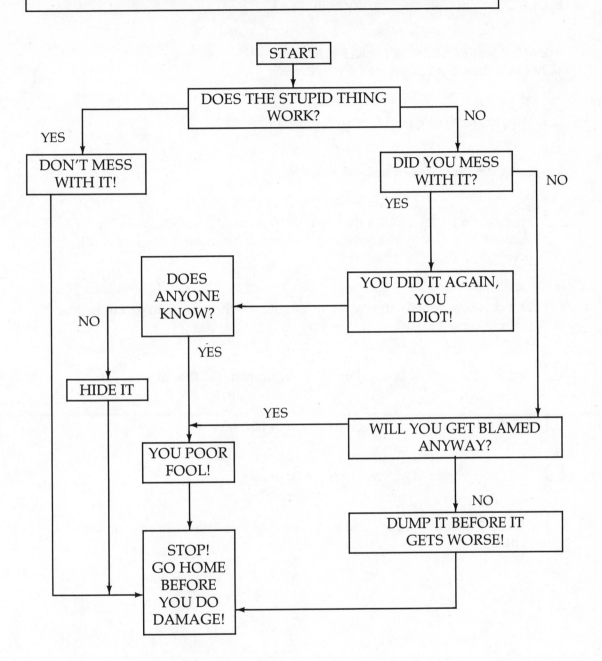

REVIEW OF SECTION VI

HUMOR KEEPERS WORTH KEEPING
(Check the box if you agree)

☐ People like to hire people with a sense of humor.

☐ Laughter increases as social density increases.

☐ Humor is a bridge builder that puts a "positive deposit" in your "people account"—It gives you something to borrow on when change or conflict occurs.

☐ The cheapest benefit on any job is laughter—When fun is allowed, people want to come to work.

☐ Laugh with instead of at others—"It reminds me of the time I..."

☐ Send "Humor Grams" to give the gift of laughter.

☐ Look in a mirror—Get your face out of park!

☐ Make a "Laughter Spot" and a "Humor Album" part of your corporate culture.

USING THE FUNNY SIDE TO IMPROVE SALES

''Everybody lives by selling something.''

Robert Louis Stevenson

''It's no coincidence that the man I know who always has the best stock of new jokes is not a comedian, but a salesman.''

John Cleese

''Show me some cartoons! ''I'm sick of numbers, and I could use a laugh!'' That statement by a health care executive speaks to a need many often feel. Everyone seems overly concerned about numbers and justifying purchases. But people also need something to break that tension. They won't buy without the numbers, but when the choice is close, they usually go with people that bring them ''joy.''

''You sales representatives are always pushing for a sale!'' That reply by a purchasing agent invited an unexpected response. The experienced saleswoman and long time contact, pulled out her business card and showed it to the agent. ''See. It says 'Sales Representative.' Yeah, I'm trying to sell you something. I thought you knew that. I'll try my best to never sell you something you don't need, but I'm here to sell.'' Now the agent was smiling. She went on to grasp his card and read back to him. ''Your card says 'Purchasing Manager.' I'll do what I do best—sell. Why don't you do what you do best—purchase.''

Everyone is in sales in one form or another. If you can build a bridge to create a sense of ''this person is one of us'', you are on the road to building a career. Successful organizations are constantly trying to build a rationale to get others to buy a product, a service, a proposal, or an idea. Humor can break down sales resistance for car dealers, insurance, real estate and door-to-door salespeople. Humor that is drawn from the situation can be used to establish rapport and break the early tension in sales situations. It can be used as an unexpected event to bring back attention and help transition your sales effort.

Humorous anecdotes can also be used to paint vivid pictures of customer needs, product benefits, or examples of legendary service. Humor gives your sales presentations a human touch and makes your products, services and ideas come to life. Will you look silly sometimes? Yes, it is better to look silly and sell, than look conventional and go broke.

HUMOR HELPS MAKE THE SALE

Malcolm L. Kushner, a humor consultant, suggested a one-two-three approach to effectively use humor in sales. He recommends using a set-up with two straight messages followed by a third that is humorous and unexpected. "Our product is safe from radiation and safe from electrical overload. But it won't clean ovens."

Can advertising mislead consumers? Yes. The method works for some but in the long haul it is necessary to meet customer needs for quality products and service or the "joke" will be on you. Customers are "entertained" by companies who don't provide what they promise. The product must perform in a realistic, honest way. Even in humor, there is never a justification for misrepresentation.

Humor can be of a significant help when it is necessary to discuss painful topics like collections. One sales representative told a delinquent account, "We appreciate your business, but give us a break. Your account is overdue ten months. This means we've carried you longer than your mother did."

Humor will never substitute for an effective sales technique. You must still know your product, probe, listen, and close. But you may end up hearing a comment similar to: "I can't remember when I have had so much fun while spending so much."

**Humor is more effective than doing
this to make a sale**

HUMOROUS ADVERTISING IS BIG BUCKS BECAUSE IT WORKS

''Humorous advertising is doing the job. The consumer has so many distractions, so much to do, so much information clamoring for his attention, that off-beat advertising is about the only decent way of getting and holding his attention.''

John Martins

''There isn't anything you can't sell with humor. An important must, however, is a client with a strong sense of humor. We never make fun of the product, but we do have fun with the product. The image of the product must not take a beating. Rather the product and the advertiser acquire likability.''

''Laughter and good humor are the canaries in the mine of commerce. If you and your employees, customers and vendors don't have a good time, if the laughter has died, you're in the wrong business.''

Tips from a Maverick Entrepreneur

On television and radio we are bombarded daily with large doses of advertising humor designed to get your attention and sell you a product or service. Don't limit yourself to the big budget advertising agencies; learn from sales representatives that have learned to use humor.

"We have clothing for every lifestyle"

Strategies That Work

One tire sales rep frequently used this favorite payoff line, ''I skid you not.''

One humor author said on a talk show that he hoped his book ''becomes a jest seller.''

A life insurance agent surprised by the low coverage a client was carrying said, ''You don't plan on staying dead long, do you?''

An enterprising journalism student put himself through school by going to companies that might use his skills and asked, ''do you need an editor? A reporter? A copy boy?'' When the all too familiar reply would be, ''We don't have any openings right now,'' he would pull out a ''No Help Needed'' sign and say ''Then you need one of these!'' He almost always got the organization to take a sign. Even more important, he strategically positioned his name and number on the back of each sign with the admonition—''When you do need someone, call me first!'' His humorous sign effectively communicated a message—''Hey, I'm different and fun.'' He received several interviews.

A charming Bed and Breakfast treated guests to style and humor. On one wall was the sign, ''Henri Matisse, Carmen Miranda, Ernest Hemmingway and Errol Flynn. . .never slept here. Given the chance they would have.''

A local bank, tired of their stodgy image decided to liven things up. A painting on the side of the bank showed an alien flying saucer that had crashed into the bank. The back doors of the four bank vans showed the following scenes: Two card-playing convicts (one of whom is cheating); masked men cracking a vault; counterfeiters inspecting their bills; and a washing machine in which money is being laundered. People enjoyed a brief laugh and remembered the bank.

A pharmaceutical representative shared her ''Rules for Sales Success'' on the back of a business card: 1. Never shake hands with a microbiologist; 2. Take no prisoners! 3. Don't be afraid to screw up; 4. Never ride generic elevators; 5. The only well managed company is your competitor; and 6. All accountants are enemies.''

Will humor work with every employer or contact—nothing works all the time, but ask yourself, ''Does it work with you?'' Most people are people; with some you just have to dig to find their funny bone. Humor can increase your sales batting average; learn to make room for it in your approach.

GETTING THROUGH TO SELL

Every sales representative knows the importance of getting through the myriad of screeners and secretaries to get to the sales prospect. Humor works in getting cooperation. It is prudent to use humor in building positive bridges to support staff rather than trying to get around them. If they are your ally, they can often make your sale. The next time you run into a surly screener take a try at humor.

Strategies That Work

''Don't tell me. I bet I'm the twentieth call you've had this morning.''

''If I'm the interruption that interrupted your last interruption, I promise to keep it brief.''

''Try being like a disc jockey by saying: 'I'm sorry you're only the fourth caller! Please try again.' ''

''We both know the best gift you can give someone is to cancel a meeting. Look, if you'll give me another appointment later this week, I'll stop pestering you now.''

Write humorous notes on the outside of your letters. Try, ''PLEASE OPEN BEFORE READING.''

Whatever you say or write, let your smile shine through. Send cards, humorous cartoons, or promotional gifts to the screeners and secretaries that make your work easy. They deserve your support and appreciation. Keeping humor working for you can help you get through the gatekeeper time and time again.

THE HUMOR CLOSE

Humor not only builds rapport and open doors; it also helps close sales.

STRATEGIES THAT WORK

One salesperson collected humorous anecdotes to counter and work through frequent objections. When a prospect wasn't interested, the salesperson would smile and say, ''That's what Charlie said, and now he's one of our best customers. Charlie was sure it wouldn't. . . .'' He would share a short anecdote illustrating the way that proposed problem proved to be no obstacle. He continued his approach in countering each objection after laughing, ''That's what. . .said, but he now uses our product and swears by it. . .'' Every objection the prospect voiced became a humorous remembrance that dealt with the objection.

Another representative frequently took the polish off of a normally professional image and laughed with clients. He called it his ''drop the briefcase close.'' In the process of his presentation, he'd drop his briefcase and say, ''It's been one of those days. Do you ever have any of those?'' He'd use the common ground to get identification and break down the distance. He found that self-depreciating humor often worked wonders.

Most people are so saturated with marketing, advertising and sales pressure, that they are resistant to influence. Humor allows a salesperson to grab the shirt of a customer and say, ''I've got something different.'' It should sell, not just entertain. A comic is successful when entertaining, but a salesperson is effective only when humor helps sell the product or service. Don't take the spotlight off of your product or service. Your humorous stories should enhance your product's benefits. Make it a habit to give the facts clearly and keep the humor secondary. Humor is the sweetner clustered either at the beginning to get attention, or at the end to provide a pleasant witticism. Humor enhances persuasion and reduces sales resistance. Using humor improperly can negatively affect a favorable perception of a product if the humor is in questionable taste. Be selective about your use of humor—humanize without ever putting people down.

Never associate your product or service with a ''negative'' for the sake of humor. Keep your humor warm and believable. Is this a product, a service, or a company that people can accept as fun? If the humor you use does not leave clients with that perception, don't use the humor.

Guidelines for Keeping Sales Humor Effective

How does this anecdote relate to my concern? Identify quickly the facts that build the setting for the story and explain why you are telling it.

How do I get them to empathize? You want your listener to say "That's me!" If they don't see it as having happened to them, they have to believe it could happen. They want to know how the surprise ending helps your product or service get them out of the problem.

Where's the benefit? You want the listener to say, "That's great!" Something about the product helps the customer out of the problem.

Where's the twist? You need a payoff line that resolves the problem in a humorous way and leaves you both laughing. Try and keep it warm and positive.

What's your exit line? Humor that is effective is quick. Develop transition statements that move you back to your sales presentation. Don't belabor the humor. Pace your sales call by moving back to a more serious discussion of the benefits of the product.

EXERCISE: Develop Two Humorous Anecdotes that Refute Objections You Frequently Hear

Take the time to look for anecdotes all the time. Finding a good anecdote should excite you as much as stumbling onto new product benefits. Anecdotes help bring product or service benefits alive! List two you use already:

1. _____

   _____

2. _____

   _____

EXERCISE: List Two Humorous Examples That Show Legendary Service

Keeping customers today requires providing quality customer service. Many examples of your organization's legendary service are ripe for producing humorous anecdotes that new clients will remember and appreciate. Take time to list some of your humorous examples of service above and beyond the call of duty:

1. _____

2. _____

BUILD RAPPORT WITH HUMOR

Humor appeals to a sense of enjoyment rather than a sense of logic. Know the numbers and have the product information, but your sales efforts should approach an individual's mind, emotions, and funny bone. You can't reason with people who aren't paying attention.

Strategies That Work

One Traffic School (required for certain ticketed drivers) has learned to make something unpleasant both fun and effective. The owners found that their most effective teachers were the funniest. They then hired professional comedians, trained them as driving teachers, and watched sales jump 50%. Today, 40 comedian/teachers keep 5,000 students chuckling each month, while learning a serious lesson.

One major organization hired a troupe of life-size puppets to help sell at conventions. One prospect told them, ''How can you turn away a talking eagle with a 12-foot wingspan?''

Most people love cartoons. Cartoon ads consistently receive high scores in recall studies. If you send product information, don't be afraid to include a personalized cartoon that targets your service or product. Most cartoon ads use a caption to provide the humor. The drawing, though fun to look at, should not be outrageous. People will identify with positive, witty, and friendly characters. Poke fun, but be gentle. A good cartoon won't say it all, it just invites people to pay attention, to your ad text.

At the suggestion of a marketing consultant, a cracker company found a way to get their distributors to read company updates. They communicate important company information between articles about Bigfoot and aliens in a quarterly parody. One headline got the message across—''Distributor Comes Back From the Dead...To Collect Bonus''.

REVIEW OF SECTION VII

HUMOR KEEPERS WORTH KEEPING
(Check those with which you agree)

☐ Everyone in an organization is in sales.

☐ Humor breaks down sales resistance.

☐ Humor can be used as an unexpected event to focus attention and help transition your sales effort.

☐ Humorous anecdotes can also be used to paint vivid pictures of customer needs, product benefits, and examples of legendary service.

☐ Humor gives a sales presentation a human touch and makes products, services and ideas come to life.

☐ Even in humor, there is no justification for misrepresentation.

☐ It is never a good idea to make fun of the product. But it is a great idea to have fun with the product.

☐ Humor will help get past ''gatekeepers'' and surly screeners.—Don't be difficult, be funny.

☐ Short humorous anecdotes will handle sales objections by showing how problems can be overcome.

☐ Humor should be secondary to your product or service benefits.

☐ Never associate your product or service with ''negative'' humor.

"The skills of exaggeration, reversal, association, spontaneity, juxtaposition and paradox are all involved in creativity and humor."

Norman Cousins

HUMOR FACTOR AND CREATIVITY

S_EC_TI_ON
VIII

''People who don't laugh at work fall into tunnel vision. They are not as open to creative solutions.''

Joel Goodman

''Humor happens when two worlds collide. Something unexpected has to happen that jolts you up and out of the normal pattern and then you start laughing. Humor is the synapse between the regular and the surprising. Every time we laugh, we are making a leap between two worlds.

Margie Brown, author *Theology of Clowning*

HUMOR AND CREATIVITY

We were taught that adults are supposed to be serious. Unfortunately, such early parent training runs contrary with some recent research on the importance of playfulness and humor. Ann Marstin, at the University of Minnesota, found that the top children in intelligence and social skills in grades 4-8, also had the best sense of humor. We can't leave that sense of humor with the children. Adults are required to be more and more creative on the job. In a changing world we need to be open to ''fooling around'' with ideas to explore new mental connections. Playfulness and humor helps develop flexible thinking. Humor is a brainteaser that can stir up new perspectives. We live in an age that requires change, innovation, and creativity.

Avner Ziv's research in Israel suggests that participation in a humorous experience before a brainstorming session increases creativity and ''divergent thinking.'' Humor helps promote innovation by making it legitimate to think in imperfect and illogical ways.

As with any creative activity, judgement during humor exercises should be suspended while the creative process is flowing. Being too self-critical will inhibit the full expression of ideas. In your brainstorming meetings, express and write down anything that comes to your mind. Unproductive ideas can be thrown out later. Don't censor before ideas are expressed; let things flow. Promote a history of persistence. When Thomas Edison was asked if he ever got discouraged trying to invent the light bulb. He replied, ''No, I found 5000 ways how not to make a light bulb. Every one was intriguing.''

Strategies That Work

One manager uses juggling to teach her staff about learning. She has her staff throw two tennis balls into the air and let them drop. She then teaches the secret of juggling—focus on the process, not the result of catching the balls. Catching works by itself when the process is in balance. Jugglers learned that if they remained relaxed as the balls landed in their hands, they were automatically caught. She pointed out the parallels between juggling and creative problem solving and change. During change, it is important to relax and trust your mind to learn when given the opportunity to practice and explore new skills.

Tired of the same old rut during staff meetings, a manager ended a meeting early and asked the staff to try viewing the meeting as a game. Their goal was to figure out the objectives of the game; the skills needed by the players; and the rules of the game. They tried to determine how a ''winner'' was determined. It provided a different, fun opportunity to view their meetings. Many requested some constructive changes in the rules of the ''game.''

A facilitator helped an engineering group prepare for a project proposal presentation to upper management. She asked the question, ''How would an ad agency sell your proposal?'' ''What music, slogans, or advertisements would your proposal inspire and what does this say about your approach to your presentation?''

A successful middle manager wanted to keep his managers flexible and keep his mind open to new ideas. Every meeting he made it a habit to prepare a new ''What if...'' question to stimulate discussion. Many were humorous.

"Be creative when conducting meetings"

TAKE TIME TO BE OUTRAGEOUS

> "Ruts are coffins with the ends kicked out of them."
>
> *Anonymous*

In our changing world it is difficult to generate a creative environment that fosters innovation. One manager put it succinctly, "The hardest thing I have to do is prepare my people for their obsolescence. By the time we have produced a new product, someone else out there is making it obsolete. We constantly have to create a sense of creative dissatisfaction." Humor and playfulness helps provide a painless way to do that. When people see others doing things differently and enjoying their work, they get permission to do the same. Learning to break out of ruts can start when you cultivate the unexpected in your life.

Cultivate the Outrageous

Make faces in a mirror daily.

Stick out your tongue at unexpected moments.

Pay for the person behind you at a tollbooth.

Face the rear in an elevator.

Have a group of your colleagues stare up and point while waiting in line.

Play tasteful practical jokes.

On occasion, take things literally and do exactly what you are told, (i.e., "drop everything.") When you act out a secondary meaning of a message humor is the result.

EXERCISES: Being Outrageous Your Way

List two outrageous things you could do this week on or off the job.

1. _____

2. _____

CARTOON EXERCISE

EXERCISES: The Cartooning Advantage

Take this cartoon and develop your own caption.

Here's a funny caption; draw your own cartoon.

''Say! Look what they're doing!''

For an innovative cartooning experience, take pictures of team members in funny situations on the job. Post them on your humor bulletin board with blank post-it's below each. Invite workers to write their own captions for the pictures. Whenever you see a great cartoon, cover the caption and make up your own.

HUMOR EXERCISES

EXERCISE: "You know it's been a bad day when..."

"You turn on the TV and they are showing emergency routes out of the city."

"Your horn goes off and remains stuck as you follow a group of tough looking motorcyclists on a deserted freeway."

"You see a local news team waiting for you at your car.'

Try your own:

1. _____

2. _____

EXERCISE: "Don't you hate it when..."

"You get put on hold when you are calling long distance."

"When you buy a new outfit and spill grease on it the first time it's used."

Add your own below:

1. _____

2. _____

You know it's a bad day when you
get the wrong date for the office party

62

HUMOR EXERCISES (Continued)

EXERCISE: Develop a workable "Candid Camera" episode you could use on the job.

Try thinking of candid camera situations that would work in your office. Develop ideas that come to life quickly, that hold the attention of viewers and participants, and bring a laugh. Candid Camera routines tended to use one of the following types of episodes. Try doing the same.

Reversing Normal or Anticipated Procedures: (Try an unusual elevator riding procedure.)

_____

Deal with Surprises: (Remember the mechanic that was asked to check the engine, but it was gone or the mailbox that talked)

_____

Something that makes sense in one area but not another: (Develop a sign that fits in one location, but not where it is placed, i.e., the sign when entering Delaware read "closed today".)

_____

EXERCISE: Write a Silly Work Song

"Push, push, push yourself everywhere you go. Hurry, hurry, hurry, hurry—got to get that dough!"　　　　　　　(Row, row, row your boat)

A group of CPA's in Philadelphia celebrate April 15th doing a "Briefcase Brigade" strut-and-chant show at a local disco. Their rap song: "I don't care what people say. I just want to be a CPA. I don't care for rock n' roll. Rather find a tax loophole."

Write your Own:

_____

_____

HUMOR EXERCISES (Continued)

EXERCISE: Cliche Challenges

''If your cup runneth over, **just get yourself another cup.**''

''I couldn't wait for success, **so I went ahead without it**.''

''I'm glad to be here. **I'm glad to be anywhere.**''

''If at first you don't succeed, **you are running about average**.''

Take one of the following cliches and add an added twist to develop humor:

''You took the words right out of my mouth.''

''He has money to burn.''

''Out of sight, Out of mind.''

''She'll try anything once.''

''Stop me if you heard this one.''

''Oh, I can't complain.''

''It was a slip of the tongue.''

EXERCISE: The Exaggeration Game

Practice taking statements to the extreme and bringing humor into your conversations.

''I'm so nervous, my butterflies have turned to eagles.''

''I was so nervous, my knees were knocking. When I asked for feedback, one person in the front said, 'I don't know. I couldn't really hear what you were saying. The drummer in the other room was playing too loudly.' ''

Try your own:

''My . . . . was so . . . .''

1. _____

2. _____

3. _____

Thomas Edison had a desk full of humorous quips. He put humorous sayings in the margins of his experiment notebooks to lighten the load of his assistants. Albert Einstein and Buckminster Fuller were also known for their sharp wits. It may not be a coincidence that some of the most creative minds in history had a good sense of humor.

REVIEW OF SECTION VIII

HUMOR KEEPERS WORTH KEEPING
(Check those with which you agree)

☐ Play around—Humor and playfulness promote creativity.

☐ Participation in a humorous experience before a creative brainstorming session increases creativity and "divergent thinking."

☐ Don't censor ideas during creative sessions—Let humorous ideas flow.

☐ Set aside a corner of your "Humor Bulletin Board" for creativity.

☐ Cultivate the unexpected to get people out of their ruts. Generate creative dissatisfaction.

☐ Some of the most creative minds in history had a good sense of humor.

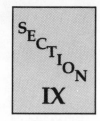

LAUGHTER MAY BE
THE BEST MEDICINE

"All the days of the afflicted are bad, but a cheerful heart has a continual feast."
Proverbs 15:15 (New Amercian Standard Bible)

"Death is nature's way of telling us to slow down."
Anonymous

One of the best uses of humor is it's value in handling the stress of our crazy world. Laughter is a non-fattening, contagious, pleasant tranquilizer without side effects. It can help people live longer, healthier lives, and recover more quickly from stress-related illnesses. Humor provides counterbalance. It is an "inner upper," a "mental recess," an ever present safety valve, and one of the most effective stress breaks available.

"Laughter interrupts the panic cycle of an illness."
Norman Cousins

Although humor may not be a cure for cancer, there is clinical evidence that laughter can mobilize our body defenses and reduce pain. In their healing centers, ancient Greeks included a visit to the "home of comedians" as part of their "therapeia process". Research supports that laughter is a natural tranquilizer. There is a direct correlation between laughter and levels of catecholamines in the blood which cause the release of endorphins in our brain. Endorphins are nature's best built-in pain killer.

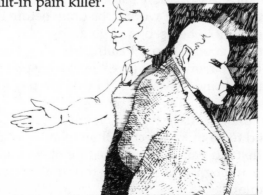

Attitude and humor have a direct relation to how we feel

LAUGHTER MAY BE THE BEST MEDICINE
(Continued)

"The art of medicine consists of amusing the patient while nature cures the disease."

Voltaire

"Warning: Laughter may be hazardous to your illness."

Nurses for Laughter

"Three to five minutes of intense laughter can double the heart rate—the aerobic equivalent of three strenuous minutes on a rowing machine!"

Dr. William Fry, Jr.

"When we laugh, muscles are activated. When we stop laughing, these muscles relax. Since muscle tension magnifies pain, many people with arthritis, rheumatism and other painful conditions benefit greatly from a healthy dose of laughter."

Dr. William Fry, Jr.

"Over the years, I have encountered a surprising number of instances in which, to all appearances, patients have laughed themselves back to health, or at least have used their sense of humor as a very positive and adaptive response to their illness. There is an inverse relationship between humor and pain."

Raymond A. Moody, Jr.

But there are those that doubt this ho-ho-holistic medicine. Art Bouchwald reacted to the American Medical Association's article on the importance of laughter. He wrote: "There is still a lot of work to be done before the food and drug administration will permit it to be used in large doses. Many unanswered questions remain, if laughter is good for your health, why don't doctors ever laugh when they are with their patients? Is it possible to transplant a sense of humor? If it is so good as a medicine, why doesn't medicare pay for it?"

Maybe we ought to change the old adage to say, "It only hurts when you don't laugh." Laughter was found to be more effective than relaxation training in increasing the ability to withstand pain. Even in the face of serious disease, there are choices to make. A person diagnosed as having terminal cancer can fight for life or usher in his or her funeral.

USING URGENCY BREAKERS

The amount of stress experienced in any situation is largely a perception of the event. The same situation can create panic in one person and generate laughter from another. Well placed humor can break the urgency cycle and create a different, less stressful, perception. It's the dead serious types that drop dead; they live in a continual state of pressure. Just because we are miserable doesn't mean we can't enjoy our lives. Instead of being consumed with crises, some people learn to roll good-naturedly with what life gives them. "Urgency breakers" can help you provide that perspective wherever you are; they "reframe" even the most frustrating moments. We can learn to reframe stress into an opportunity. When you realize that the past is finished and you can laugh about it, you are free to bounce back and get busy fixing the problem or preparing for what to do the next time it happens. Do any of these "urgency breakers" sound familiar?

URGENCY BREAKERS THAT WORK

"Some days you're the bug, some days the windshield"

"You win some, you lose some."

"The crisis of today is the boring history of tomorrow."

"Are we having fun yet?"

"This too shall pass."

"Some days are for hanging on."

"It could be worse; I could be pregnant."

"Some days the dragon wins."

"I've got one nerve left. How'd you find it?"

"You want it when?"

"Nothing is perfect"

"The only light at the end of the tunnel is a train coming the   other way."

"I can't believe I really did that!"

"Keep the razor blades away from me for a minute please."

"Life is hard, then you die."

EXERCISE: Write Your Two Favorite "Urgency Breakers"

1. _____

2. _____

KEEPING YOUR HUMOR PERSPECTIVE

Perspective is vital. Sometimes it takes more than one statement to build the effect. This abbreviated letter from a student to her parents helps hammer home the point of keeping things in perspective better than any explanation could.

Dear Mom and Dad:

I'm sorry for not writing, but hope you will understand. First, sit down before you read further.

I'm doing much better now after recovering from the concussion I received jumping from my dorm window when it caught fire last month. I can almost see normally thanks to the loving care of Norman, the janitor who pulled me from the flames. He more than saved me; he's become my whole life. I have been living with him since the fire. We are planning on getting married. We haven't got a date yet, but plan to have one soon, before my pregnancy shows.

Yes, I'm pregnant. I know you would be excited for me, knowing how much you want to be grandparents. We'd be married now, if it weren't for Norman's infection that prevented him passing the premarital blood test. I caught it from him, but the doctors are positive it won't affect the child.

Although not well-educated, I know your often-expressed tolerance will make it easy for you to accept Norm.

Your loving daughter

Susie

P.S. There was no fire. I have no concussion. I'm not pregnant, and there is no Norman. However, I'm getting an "F" in Biology and wanted you to see that grade in its proper perspective.

EXERCISE: Handling Your Worry List

There are many strategies that use humor to promote a more realistic perspective in the face of your next crisis. Take a moment to list three concerns you have; make it your own "Worry List" from your life.

1. _____

2. _____

3. _____

Find a coworker or friend and take the time to share your worries. But end each worry with "Ho-ho-ho," "Ha-ha-ha," "Tee-hee," or "Hee-hee-hee." Watch your concerns diminish with the laughter that is generated.

HUMOR STRESS BREAKS

It is all to easy to forgo breaks in our hectic, competitive workplace. The stress management literature suggests that three short ''stress breaks'' daily are adequate to bring workers out of the ''rat race'' and into ''relaxation.'' Humor can make stress breaks even more effective. Keep your team well supplied with ''fun-raisers.''

HUMOR LIBRARIES TO THE RESCUE

Develop a humor library of books and tapes. Pick a location where people can relax, get rejuventated and refreshed. Such places are usually bright spaces with cartoons, comic posters, books, board games, and popular audio and video tapes. In our highly stressful and competitive work environments we need rooms to help provide counterbalance. Make a list of the magazines that your staff likes, and make them available.

Humor Comes to the Rescue

Sometimes there's no time to plan, and canned phrases can't do the situation justice. When you cultivate the humor edge, the ''poppers'' will come when most needed.

One worker trying to bring humor into a boring low calorie lunch, ceremoniously faced a banana about to be devoured and said, ''Prepare to die.''

In the face of unexpected turbulence, a worried first-time flyer asked an experienced flyer in the next seat, ''Are we going to get down OK?'' The answer was with a smile, ''Well, to my knowledge, they've never left anyone up here.'' Their laugh together helped break the tension.

''Die young as late as possible. That way you'll live longer.''
Ashley Montagu

''He who laughs; lasts.''
Anonymous

Here's hoping you last too, and that you laugh a little along the way for fun and profit.

REVIEW OF SECTION IX

HUMOR KEEPERS WORTH KEEPING
(Check the box if you agree)

☐ Laughter is a non-fattening, contagious, pleasant tranquilizer without side effects.

☐ Laughter can interrupt the panic cycle of an illness and acutally promote healing.

☐ Well placed humor can break the urgency cycle and create a different, less stressful, perception.

☐ ''Urgency breakers'' can help shift even the most frustrating moments into opportunities.

☐ Share your worries—End with ''Ho-ho-ho,'' ''Ha-ha-ha,'' or ''Hee-hee-hee.'' Then get busy investing wasted ''worrytime'' into constructive actions.

☐ He who laughs; lasts—Humor may be the best medicine.

SECTION X

REVIEW OF HUMOR

HUMOR KEEPERS WORTH KEEPING

Let's take one more look at humor keepers that are worth keeping. Put a check mark next to the statements you most want to work on. Take the time to go back to sections and make a list of specific quotes and examples that illustrate and explain the concept. If you take time once a week to review that information you will have formed a new habit that will help you make humor work for you on the job.

SECTION I: TAKING YOUR JOB SERIOUSLY AND YOURSELF LIGHTLY

☐ When humor is working, you laugh with people, not at them.

☐ Don't hide in humor; use it.

☐ Take your job seriously and yourself lightly.

☐ Take time to relive your humor history.

☐ Work the funny side by using ''the lifters'' and ''the poppers.''

☐ Keep your humor history where you can find it—your laughter log, humor file, and humor album.

☐ Trade Perfection, Procrastination, Paralysis for Practice, Practice, Practice.

☐ Ask ''Does it work?'' not ''Is it funny?''

SECTION II: SELF-CONFIDENCE AND THE ABILITY TO LAUGH AT YOURSELF

☐ Don't take yourself too seriously.

☐ Laughter provides perspective getting us quickly out of the rearview mirror and back into constructive action.

☐ Self-depreciating humor humanizes the speaker—''He's one of us!''

☐ Humor helps promote a coping model of management that supports early problem solving.

☐ Don't worry about humor that ''bombs''—Use ''savers'' to capitalize on your misfortune.

REVIEW OF HUMOR (Continued)

SECTION III: THE COMMUNICATION EDGE: BALANCING SUBSTANCE WITH STYLE

☐ Communicate with substance and style.

☐ Good communicators touch their listeners in three ways—their heart, their brain, and their funnybone.

☐ Give 'AhHa's' through 'HaHa's.''

☐ Humorous illustrations provide ''attention grabbers'' and ''memory hooks'' for retention.

☐ Practice won't make you perfect, just better.

☐ Tell one joke or story a week to every person you have time to talk to.

☐ Keep your humor brief and fast-paced.

☐ Work at both the set-up and the punchline.

☐ Master the pause.

☐ Allow yourself to be silly.

☐ Keep using your ''winners.''

☐ If you must use sexual, ethnic, or questionable humor, keep it off the job.

☐ Use a ''humor sandwich''—Tell it serious; tell it funny; tell it serious.

☐ Keep your humor on target—Use the common transition statements, ''Speaking of . . .'' or ''That reminds me of . . .''

SECTION IV: DISARMING ANGER WITH HUMOR

☐ You don't get rid of conflict in a dynamic, changing world—use it.

☐ Behind every angry person's attack is a problem that needs to be dealt with.

☐ Instead of using counterattacks or defensiveness, ''verbal aikido'' uses positive empathetic humor to defuse verbal attacks.

☐ When attacked, accept, redirect, and affirm.

☐ Disarming anger should not be used to avoid problem solving.

☐ Develop and use comebacks that turn snarls to smiles in even the toughest customers.

☐ Don't hide in humor—Use it to promote problem solving.

REVIEW OF HUMOR (Continued)

SECTION V: MAKING HUMOR WORK FOR CHANGE

☐ Resistance goes along with the territory whenever change occurs.

☐ Not all resistance is bad; some changes should never even occur.

☐ Resistance needs to be honored, listened to, and dealt with.

☐ Use humor to handle the early discomfort of change—Laughing together allows all to say, "We're all in this together, and we're all uncomfortable."

☐ When you rest, you rust.

☐ Don't leave humor to chance in changing times—Plan for it!

SECTION VI: USING HUMOR TO BUILD BRIDGES AND TEAMWORK

☐ People like to hire people with a sense of humor.

☐ Laughter increases as social density increases.

☐ To be effective, managers need a 4 to 1 positive to negative contact ratio.

☐ Humor is a bridge builder that puts a "positive deposit" in your "people account"—It gives you something to borrow on when change or conflict occurs.

☐ The cheapest benefit on any job is laughter—When fun is allowed, people want to come to work.

☐ Laugh with instead of at others—"It reminds me of the time I..."

☐ Send "Humor Grams" to give the gift of laughter.

☐ Look in a mirror—Get your face out of park!

☐ Make a "Laughter Spot" and a "Humor Album" part of your corporate culture.

SECTION VII: USING THE FUNNY SIDE FOR SALES PROFIT

☐ Everyone in an organization is in sales.

☐ Humor breaks down sales resistance.

☐ Humor can be used as an unexpected event to focus attention and help transition your sales effort.

REVIEW OF HUMOR (Continued)

SECTION VII—CONTINUED

- [ ] Humorous anecdotes can also be used to paint vivid pictures of customer needs, product benefits, and examples of legendary service.

- [ ] Humor gives a sales presentation a human touch and makes products, services and ideas come to life.

- [ ] Even in humor, there is no justification for misrepresentation.

- [ ] It is never a good idea to make fun of the product. But it is a great idea to have fun with the product.

- [ ] Humor will help you get past "gatekeepers" and surly screeners.—Don't be difficult, be funny.

- [ ] Short humorous anecdotes will handle sales objections by showing how problems can be overcome.

- [ ] Humor should be secondary to your product or service benefits.

- [ ] Never associate your product or service with "negative" humor.

SECTION VIII: HUMOR FACTOR AND INNOVATION

- [ ] Play around—Humor and playfulness promote creativity.

- [ ] Participation in a humorous experience before a creative brainstorming session increases creativity and "divergent thinking."

- [ ] Don't censor ideas during creative sessions.—Let ideas flow.

- [ ] Set aside a corner of your "Humor Board" for creativity.

- [ ] Cultivate the unexpected to get people out of their ruts. Generate creative dissatisfaction.

- [ ] Some of the most creative minds in history had a good sense of humor.

SECTION IX: LAUGHTER MAY BE THE BEST MEDICINE

- [ ] Laughter is a non-fattening, contagious, pleasant tranquilizer without side effects.

- [ ] Laughter can interrupt the panic cyle of an illness and actually promote healing.

- [ ] Well placed humor can break the urgency cycle and create a different, less stressful, perception.

- [ ] "Urgency breakers" can help shift even the most frustrating moments into opportunities.

- [ ] Share your worries—End with "Ho-ho-ho," "Ha-ha-ha," or "Hee-hee-hee." Then get busy investing wasted "worrytime" into constructive actions.

- [ ] He who laughs; lasts—Humor may be the best medicine!

APPENDIX: REFERENCES

HUMOR WORKS REFERENCES

Adler, Joey, *Jokes and How to Tell Them*. Doubleday, New York 1963.

Baily, Janet, ''Rx: Laughter,'' *McCall's* August, 1988, pp. 106-107.

Bletcher, William, MD, *Intimate Play*. Viking Press, New York 1987.

Black, Donald W. MD, ''Laughter,'' *Journal of American Medical Association*, Dec. 7, 1984, V.252, N. 21, pp. 2995-2998. (excellent Medical reference list).

Bloch, Arthur, *Murphy's Law*, Price Stern & Sloan Publishers, Los Angeles, 1970, 1980, 1982 (Vol 1-3).

Blumenfeld, Esther, and Alpern, Lynne, *The Smile Connection: How to Use Humor in Dealing with People*. Simon & Schuster, New York 1987.

Fagan, Pete and Schaffer, *The Office Humor Book*. Crown Publishers, New York 1985.

Fisher, Russ, *In Search of the Funny Bone*. 1085 Capital Club Circle N.E., Atlanta, GA 30319.

Forman, Michael, ''Making Light of Business'' The *American Way*, March 15, 1988, pp. 41-44.

Funt, Allan, ''Laugh Where We Must, Be Candid Where We Can,'' *Psychology Today* (Interview), June 1985, pp. 43-47.

Goodman, Joel, *Laughing Matters*. The Humor Project, Sagamore Institute, 110 Spring St., Saratoga Springs, NY 12866 (518) 587-8770.

Handy, Bruce and Corcoran, Alan, *Hellbent on Insanity*. P.O. Box 4586, Rockefeller Center, NY, NY 10185 ($9.95 for collection of 70's college humor).

Helitzer, Melvin, *Comedy Techniques for Writers & Performers*. Lawhead Press, Athens, Ohio, 1984.

Irvin, Dale, *Funny Business, the Humor Newsletter*. Corporate Comedy, P.O. Box 9061, Downers Grove, IL 60515 ($36/year).

APPENDIX (Continued)

Isen, Alice M., Ph.D., "How Mood Affects Creativity," *Journal of Personality and Social Psych.*, 1987, Vol. 52, pp. 1122-1131.

Klein, Allen, *The Healing Power of Humor.* J.P. Tarcher, Los Angeles, CA 1989.

Linn, Alan, "Corporate Capers", *Sky*, January 1988, pp. 84-91.

Moody, Raymond A., Jr., "Laugh After Laugh: The Healing Power of Humor," *Reader's Digest*, Feb. 1988.

Orben, Robert, *Orben's Current Comedy*, Comedy Center, 700 Orange St., Wilmington, DE 19801.

Paulson, Terry, *They Shoot Managers Don't They?*, Canter and Associates, Santa Monica, CA 90404, 1989.

Perret, Gene. *The Power of Humor for Business Speakers*, Sterling, 1988.

Peter, Laurence J., and Dana, Bill. *The Laughter Prescription.* Ballantine, New York 1982.

Raskin, Victor, "Jokes," *Psychology Today*, Oct. 1986. pp. 34-39.

Rosten, Leo. "How to Tell a Joke," *Reader's Digest*, 1985, pp. 128-130.

Tooper, Virginia, Ed. D., Editor, *Laugh Lovers News*. P.O. Box 1495, Pleasanton, CA, 94566 ($8 per year).

True, Herb, and Mang, Anna. *Humor Power: How to Get It, Give It, and Gain It.* Doubleday, Garden City, NJ, 1980. Order from Herb True, 1717 E. Colfax, South Bend, IN 46617 (219) 234-2340.

Weinstein, Matt & Goodman, Joel, *Playfair: Everyone's Guide to Noncompetitive Play.* Impact Publishers, San Luis Obispo, CA.

Wilde, Larry, *The Larry Wilde Library of Laughter.* Royal Publishing, P.O. Box 1120, Glendora, CA 91740.

Ziv, Avner, "The Influence of Humorous Atmosphere on Divergent Thinking," *Contemp. Educational Psych.*, 1983, Vol. 8, pp. 68-75. (Excellent list of references on humor and creativity).

OTHER RESOURCES

Brodnax, JoDale, The Lively Room, De Kalb General Hospital, 2701 N. Decatur Rd., Decatur, GA 30033 (Establishing a humor room in a hospital).

Caddylak Systems, Inc. 201 Montrose Rd. Westbury, NY 11590 (516) 333-8221. Humorous memos and notes, awards and certificates, headlines, and business posters that you can purchase and duplicate on the job.

The Executive Treasury of Humor (Vol. 1-4), Nightingale-Conant, 7300 N. Lehigh Ave., Chicago, IL 60648. (Actual programs by professional humorist speakers.)

Ferrari, Katherine, International Laughter Society Inc., 1600 Glen Una Drive, Los Gatos, CA 95030.

Funny Fillers, 565 Pearl St. #200, La Jolla, CA 92037. A four page newsletter with short witty items organized around each month's calendar.

HERMAN Posters, Clement Communications, Inc., Concord Industrial Park, Concordville, Penn. 19331, (800) 345-8101. Herman cartoon posters that make a point for safety and teamwork.

Klein, Allen (The Jolly-tologist), *The Whole Mirth Catalog*, 1034 Page St., San Francisco, CA 94117 (415) 431-1913 (A must for props and resources to promote humor on and off the job! Send $1 to cover catalog and postage).

Metcalf, C.W., ''The Humor Option'', video series, C.W. Metcalf & Co., 344 E. Foothills Parkway, 3-W, Fort Collins, CO 80525, 1988.

Mindess, Harvey, Antioch Humor Project, Psychology Department, Antioch University, 300 Rose Avenue, Van Ness, CA 90291.

Nilsen, Don L.F., Names and addresses of Comedy Clubs, Humor Journals, Organizations and Scholars, English Dept., Arizona State University, Tempe, AZ 85287 (602) 965-7592.

Paulson, Terry, Editor, *Management Dialogue* (Humor Corner). 28717 Colina Vista, Agoura Hills, CA 91301 (818) 991-5110 ($3 per year).

San Francisco Public Library, ''The Schmulowitz Collection of Humor''.

The Wellness Community, Harold Benjamin (founder), 1235 5th St., Santa Monica, CA 90401 (213) 393-1415.

Westcott, Jean, Funny Business, 1032 Bayview, Oakland, CA (415) 536-1657.

Wooten, Patty, RN,BS.N, ''Nancy Nurse'', 454-B Santa Clara, Alameda, CA 94501.

ABOUT THE FIFTY-MINUTE SERIES

''Every so often an idea emerges that is so simple and appealing, people wonder why it didn't come along sooner. The Fifty-Minute series is just such an idea. Excellent!''

Mahaliah Levine, Vice President for
Training and Development
Dean Witter Reynolds, Inc.

WHAT IS A FIFTY-MINUTE BOOK?

—Fifty-Minute books are brief, soft-covered, ''self-study'' titles covering a wide variety of topics pertaining to business and self-improvement. They are reasonably priced, ideal for formal training, excellent for self-study and perfect for remote location training.

''A Fifty-Minute book gives the reader fundamentals that can be applied on the job, even before attending a formal class''

Lynn Baker, Manager of Training
Fleming Corporation

WHY ARE FIFTY-MINUTE BOOKS UNIQUE?

—Because of their format. Designed to be ''read with a pencil,'' the basics of a subject can be quickly grasped and applied through a series of hands-on activities, exercises and cases.

''Fifty-Minute books are the best new publishing idea in years. They are clear, practical, concise and affordable—perfect for today's world.''

Leo Hauser, Past President
ASTD

HOW MANY FIFTY-MINUTE BOOKS ARE THERE?

—Those listed on the following pages at this time. Additional titles are always in development. For more information write to **Crisp Publications, Inc.,** **95 First Street, Los Altos, CA 94022.**

NOTES

FOR OTHER FIFTY-MINUTE SELF-STUDY BOOKS
SEE ORDER FORM AT THE BACK OF THE BOOK.

THE FIFTY-MINUTE SERIES

Quantity	Title	Code #	Price	Amount
	MANAGEMENT TRAINING			
	Successful Negotiation	09-2	$7.95	
	Personal Performance Contracts	12-2	$7.95	
	Team Building	16-5	$7.95	
	Effective Meeting Skills	33-5	$7.95	
	An Honest Day's Work	39-4	$7.95	
	Managing Disagreement Constructively	41-6	$7.95	
	Training Managers To Train	43-2	$7.95	
	The Fifty-Minute Supervisor	58-0	$7.95	
	Leadership Skills For Women	62-9	$7.95	
	Problem Solving & Decision Making	63-7	$7.95	
	Coaching & Counseling For Supervisors	68-8	$7.95	
	Management Dilemmas: A Guide to Business Ethics	69-6	$7.95	
	Understanding Organizational Change	71-8	$7.95	
	Project Management	75-0	$7.95	
	Managing Organizational Change	80-7	$7.95	
	Managing A Diverse Workforce	85-8	$7.95	
	PERSONNEL TRAINING & HUMAN RESOURCE MANAGEMENT			
	Effective Performance Appraisals	11-4	$7.95	
	Quality Interviewing	13-0	$7.95	
	Personal Counseling	14-9	$7.95	
	Job Performance and Chemical Dependency	27-0	$7.95	
	New Employee Orientation	46-7	$7.95	
	Professional Excellence for Secretaries	52-1	$7.95	
	Guide To Affirmative Action	54-8	$7.95	
	Writing A Human Resource Manual	70-X	$7.95	
	COMMUNICATIONS			
	Effective Presentation Skills	24-6	$7.95	
	Better Business Writing	25-4	$7.95	
	The Business of Listening	34-3	$7.95	
	Writing Fitness	35-1	$7.95	
	The Art of Communicating	45-9	$7.95	
	Technical Presentation Skills	55-6	$7.95	
	Making Humor Work	61-0	$7.95	
	Better Technical Writing	64-5	$7.95	
	Using Visual Aids in Business	77-7	$7.95	
	Influencing Others: A Practical Guide	84-X	$7.95	
	SELF-MANAGEMENT			
	Balancing Home And Career	10-6	$7.95	
	Mental Fitness: A Guide to Emotional Health	15-7	$7.95	
	Personal Financial Fitness	20-3	$7.95	
	Attitude: Your Most Priceless Possession	21-1	$7.95	
	Personal Time Management	22-X	$7.95	

(Continued on next page)

THE FIFTY-MINUTE SERIES

Quantity	Title	Code #	Price	Amount
	SELF-MANAGEMENT (CONTINUED)			
	Preventing Job Burnout	23-8	$7.95	
	Successful Self-Management	26-2	$7.95	
	Developing Positive Assertiveness	38-6	$7.95	
	Time Management And The Telephone	53-X	$7.95	
	Memory Skills In Business	56-4	$7.95	
	Developing Self-Esteem	66-1	$7.95	
	Creativity In Business	67-X	$7.95	
	Quality Awareness: A Personal Guide To Professional Standards	72-6	$7.95	
	Managing Personal Change	74-2	$7.95	
	Speedreading For Better Productivity	78-5	$7.95	
	Winning At Human Relations	86-6	$7.95	
	Stop Procrastinating	88-2	$7.95	
	SALES TRAINING/QUALITY CUSTOMER SERVICE			
	Sales Training Basics	02-5	$7.95	
	Restaurant Server's Guide	08-4	$7.95	
	Quality Customer Service	17-3	$7.95	
	Telephone Courtesy And Customer Service	18-1	$7.95	
	Professional Selling	42-4	$7.95	
	Customer Satisfaction	57-2	$7.95	
	Telemarketing Basics	60-2	$7.95	
	Calming Upset Customers	65-3	$7.95	
	Managing A Quality Service Organization	83-1	$7.95	
	ENTREPRENEURSHIP			
	Marketing Your Consulting Or Professional Services	40-8	$7.95	
	Starting Your Small Business	44-0	$7.95	
	Publicity Power	82-3	$7.95	
	CAREER GUIDANCE & STUDY SKILLS			
	Study Skills Strategies	05-X	$7.95	
	Career Discovery	07-6	$7.95	
	Plan B: Protecting Your Career From The Winds of Change	48-3	$7.95	
	I Got The Job!	59-9	$7.95	
	OTHER CRISP INC. BOOKS			
	Comfort Zones: A Practical Guide For Retirement Planning	00-9	$13.95	
	Stepping Up To Supervisor	11-8	$13.95	
	The Unfinished Business Of Living: Helping Aging Parents	19-X	$12.95	
	Managing Performance	23-7	$18.95	
	Be True To Your Future: A Guide to Life Planning	47-5	$13.95	
	Up Your Productivity	49-1	$10.95	
	How To Succeed In A Man's World	79-3	$7.95	
	Practical Time Management	275-4	$13.95	
	Copyediting: A Practical Guide	51-3	$18.95	

THE FIFTY-MINUTE SERIES
(Continued)

☐ Send volume discount information.

☐ Please send me a catalog.

	Amount
Total (from other side)	
Shipping ($1.50 first book, $.50 per title thereafter)	
California Residents add 7% tax	
Total	

Ship to: _____

_____

_____

_____

Phone number: _____

Bill to: _____

_____

_____

_____

P.O. # _____

All orders except those with a P.O.# must be prepaid.
For more information Call (415) 949-4888 or FAX (415) 949-1610.

NOTES

NOTES

FOR OTHER FIFTY-MINUTE SELF-STUDY BOOKS
SEE ORDER FORM AT THE BACK OF THE BOOK.